Praise for **LIONS** and **TIGERS** and Hamsters

"This book will give you insight into the animal mind and why it is important that people need animals and animals need people."

—**Temple Grandin, PhD**, author of *Animals in Translation* and *Animals Make Us Human*

"As this wonderful book proves, Dr. Mark is the rarest of veterinarians—a man who can help a family accept the loss of a beloved German shepherd one day and spar with a Siberian tiger to administer its treatment the next. Dr. Mark's deep insight into animals—his profound understanding of what they give us and what they can tell us if we're willing to listen—is an inspiration to an animal lover like me. We modeled the Annenberg PetSpace in Playa Vista on his groundbreaking work at the San Diego Humane Society. I urge everyone who cares about animals to read this delightful new volume."

—**Wallis Annenberg**, philanthropist, chairman, president, and CEO of The Annenberg Foundation

"Mark Goldstein has been a friend and colleague for almost three decades. His compassion for animals of all sizes and species—as well as his humanity—have been evident in every aspect of his esteemed career. Mark's powerful, engaging storytelling talent shines brightly throughout *Lions and Tigers and Hamsters*. This captivating book warms the heart and sometimes tickles the funny bone. But most of all, it's a celebration of wildlife and other animals by a kindhearted veterinarian who has dedicated his life to making the world a better place for all creatures."

—**Douglas G. Myers**, president and CEO, San Diego Zoo Global

"To be transported into Mark Goldstein's world, as one reads his joyous, moving, and remarkable book, is a great gift, particularly in these fractured times. *Lions and Tigers and Hamsters* allows us to temporarily remove ourselves from the world of media-generated illusions, superficialities, and demons, and discover (or rediscover) that love, in its essence, can be reaffirmed by letting the innate beauty of animals flow through us and touch our souls."

—**Peter Yarrow**, singer/songwriter, Peter, Paul and Mary

"*Lions and Tigers and Hamsters* is a wonderful journey through the life of a true champion of animal welfare. Dr. Mark Goldstein has dedicated his life to animals and has beautifully depicted the incredible stories he's lived and values he's learned in this book."

—**Robin Ganzert, PhD**, president and CEO, American Humane

"Chelsea was a lab puppy with serious health issues. Rescued by a humane society, she needed the best of veterinary care. I had just moved to Boston to work for the MSPCA. I wasn't sure where to go, but I'd heard about Mark Goldstein, who worked at Angell, the MSPCA's hospital, perhaps the best hospital in the world. Chelsea was in good hands there and she thrived. As I got to know Mark, I learned I was in good hands, too. I thrived, and I learned from Mark. Something else was special about this guy; as much as he taught, he also listened and he learned. He was a great medical person, but it was all about life where Mark really shined. He gave us all things to think about. We are all lucky that he started to write it down: all that he heard, all that he learned. This is someone worth listening to."

—**Carter Luke**, president, CEO, MSPCA-Angell

"Most of us seek to close the distance between who we are and what we do. This book is a luminous chronicle of Mark Goldstein, who has closed that gap and lived a life of unconditional love for all God's creatures. These ingredients make for a terrific read. Dr. Mark's unstinting passion for all animals domestic and wild is guaranteed to leave paw prints on your heart."

—**Richard Lederer**, bestselling author of *Anguished English*

"Dr. Mark Goldstein is a one-man example of all the jobs a veterinarian can have, from supporting dog and cat adoptions in an animal shelter to working hands-on with a rhinoceros. Truly, Goldstein has a rare ability as a writer to help you to feel as if you are in the zoo enclosure right beside him and Donia the elephant or Ralph the water buffalo or Harold the hamster. This book is a *really* engaging read for anyone who loves animals or who one day wants to be a veterinarian."

—**Steve Dale, CABC**, national radio host, *Steve Dale's Pet World* and WGN Radio Chicago; co-editor, *Decoding Your Dog*; columnist, *Veterinary Practice News* and *CATster*

LIONS and
TIGERS and
Hamsters

What Animals Large and Small Taught Me
About Life, Love, and Humanity

Mark Goldstein, DVM

Health Communications, Inc.
Deerfield Beach, Florida

www.hcibooks.com

**Library of Congress Cataloging-in-Publication Data
is available through the Library of Congress**

© 2019 Mark Goldstein, DVM

ISBN-13: 978-07573-2186-3 (Paperback)
ISBN-10: 07573-2186-0 (Paperback)
ISBN-13: 978-07573-2192-4 (ePub)
ISBN-10: 07573-2192-5 (ePub)

Publisher: Health Communications, Inc.
3201 S.W. 15th Street
Deerfield Beach, FL 33442–8190

Cover design by Larissa Hise Henoch
Interior design and formatting by Lawna Patterson Oldfield
Photos of Dr. Mark Goldstein and Ren © Janie DeCelles

CONTENTS

FOREWORD

Many of us love animals, not just companion animals, but all animals. Some love companion animals beyond dogs and cats to include birds, reptiles, and small mammals. A precious few have a deep relationship with all God's creatures: furry, feathered, and finned; warm-blooded and cold; domestic and wild; in a home and homeless. And on occasion, there enters this world a special soul who is connected with animals—with a little bit of their DNA in theirs—someone who can communicate what they've witnessed, researched, and felt to other animal lovers. I've just described my colleague, friend, and fellow author, veterinarian Mark Goldstein.

I spent years leaning in as Mark would regale friends, veterinary colleagues, and lecture attendees with his unique, detailed, and powerful stories about his experiences with animals growing up, in veterinary school, at prestigious veterinary medical centers, working in wildlife parks, major zoos, and shelters. These stories were so entertaining and motivating that the audience felt like booking a safari, going behind the scenes at a zoo, or adopting

another animal from the shelter. But a shortage of time, money, and access kept us back. Luckily, Goldstein memorialized the best of these stories in this amazing book, *Lions and Tigers and Hamsters*, allowing us to live this life through his as a practicing veterinarian, zoo director, head of a humane society, and highly influential animal advocate.

For over four decades, Mark has positively impacted the lives of pets, people, and professionals in veterinary medicine, zoos, and animal shelters. He's had a direct impact on the way society is taking better care of animals, both physically and emotionally, and done so through his unique education, training, and experience. Sometimes, it took years of hard work or moments of brute force, other times, tugging at heartstrings and a simple look moved a mountain.

In reading this book, you'll literally take a walk on the wild side, and understand in a deep soul-level way, why the human-animal bond is sacred, we should marvel at the animals we share this planet with, and double our efforts to protect them.

—Marty Becker, DVM, founder of
FearFreePets.com *and* FearFreeHappyHomes.com,
and author or coauthor of 25 pet/vet books

Caring for animals and their welfare and understanding the value of the human-animal bond is part of what makes up the fabric of a healthy community.

To those I loved but who are not here today to enjoy what they helped create:

David Zola, my lifelong friend, a gifted educator, a spiritual leader, and fun guy.

Allan and Jeanette, my loving parents, who taught me that respect and passion for life is everything.

Ren, a dog who taught me more than any other beautiful creature on Earth.

For providing inspiration, education, honest evaluation and unlimited support:

Dr. Marty Becker, making the world better, one animal and one person at a time.

Janie DeCelles, who always has my back and epitomizes what a true friend is and for taking notes. ☺

Richard Lederer, educating the world one word at a time, while making us laugh.

To those in my life without whom I would not have been inspired to share this story:

My family: Kris, Emily, Nicole, Rich, Gwen, RB, and grand-dogs Brucie and Rhone.

Loved ones and colleagues: Dr. George Myers, Marian Myers, Richard Rein, Deborah Rein, Jack Rubinstein, Jeff and Pam Goldstein, Howard and Bobbie Goldstein, Karen Taylor, Angela Smith, Dr. Michael Bernstein, Dr. Roger Thompson, Terah Collins, Sue and Richard Lamb, Dr. Richard (Dick) Lindsey, Dr. Gus Thornton, Carter Luke, Kathie Kerr, Christine Belleris, and my publisher Health Communications, Inc.

MSPCA-Angell staff, who provide compassion and care for animals and people 24/7.

To all the compassionate and dedicated staff and volunteers at veterinary hospitals, zoological parks, and humane societies that I had the honor to learn from and work with.

To my biggest fan and a great role model: Uncle Norty.

INTRODUCTION

For over forty years, I have been known as "Dr. Mark."
The title of doctor was never an ego thing or something I ever
expected to be called; it simply came with my veterinary training.
But over the years, I embraced the moniker because it represented
who I was and what I cared deeply about.

From the time I was a little boy, even before I had my first dog,
animals fascinated me. From my teens onward, I always sought
out jobs where I could learn about all creatures, domestic and
wild. Throughout college, I would spend much of my spare time
pursuing creative opportunities that provided insight into caring
for animals. I would even tag along with any veterinarian who
would let me, learning as much as possible about the art of medicine to help keep animals healthy and relieve their suffering and
pain. I just loved animals and the people who valued them.

I was fortunate enough to attend veterinary school at Cornell
University and intern at Angell Memorial Animal Hospital in
Boston, where I learned from the best minds at the most pres-
tigious animal medicine institutions in the world. From there,

my career took many turns—from working as a veterinarian in clinical practice to a director of zoos, first in Boston then in Los Angeles, and finally into the world of animal welfare as head of a progressive humane society—all of which afforded me a lifetime of experiences at the highest levels, working with all sorts of animals and people who cared for them, across a broad spectrum of animal welfare concerns.

My initial goal in sharing my stories was a selfish one. I wanted my grandchildren to know their grandpapa, and understand the lessons I learned and values I developed throughout my career.

Beyond this, as a veterinarian I felt a responsibility to advocate for the human-animal bond. That is what my stories are about—real-life experiences that celebrate the hard work done by the talented individuals who work in the world of animal welfare and shed light on the daily challenges they face, while also showing the tremendous impact that animals and their unconditional love have on our lives.

My career began in the 1970s, so many of the animal care practices described have since become outdated following great advancements made in the handling and care of animals. Similarly, the stories are real, but in some cases, names have been changed to protect privacy, or simply because some were forgotten.

My work as a veterinarian and the animals and people that I interacted with taught me how to live life. I hope this book provides insight into the world of animal care and welfare, along with a few laughs, and most importantly, hallmarks the sacred importance of the human-animal bond.

Chapter 1

DONIA

Without warning, I felt a solid leathery wall propel my body forward with such enormous force that I was lifted off my feet. It was futile to push back against such power, and I next found myself thrust high in the air, soaring forward an astonishing thirty feet before slamming into the ground at the edge of the island.

As a small boy it had irritated my mother to no end when a fly or mosquito innocently wandered into the house, and I would turn the lights off so she couldn't see to annihilate it with her swatter. Now in an ironic twist, I had become the annoying pest, and the swatter was the muscular trunk of an irritated elephant named Donia.

On the island, home to a small herd of elephants, Donia was the dominant matriarch. And although the crumpled "pest" she had so easily flicked away presented no real threat to her, she still came at me with her 12,000 pounds driven by the same nonchalant ferocity as my mother with her swatter, intent on ridding her space of an uninvited nuisance.

As soon as I landed, charging footsteps shook the ground, filling the air with a thick cloud of dust. Before I could even begin to process my dire situation, a tremendous weight came down on top of me, squeezing the air from my body.

Thanks to my training, I knew that when an elephant attacks, it will instinctively put its head down on its antagonist and raise its back feet, tipping all its weight forward and crushing the life out of its victim. This natural behavior is often used by circus elephants performing headstand tricks as a part of their act. Unfortunately for me, this was no circus trick, and I knew that, unless I managed to free myself, my veterinary career would be over before it started.

"Elephant Island" was located in Section 5 of Lion Country Safari in Loxahatchee, Florida. Loxahatchee was officially a suburb of West Palm Beach, but to me as a young adult from New York, it appeared more like a suburb of the Everglades. The safari park had opened just five years before, in 1967, as America's first drive-thru African wildlife preserve.

The grounds consisted of a 640-acre park in which hundreds of exotic animals roamed freely among visitors safely "caged" in their cars as they drove along a scenic eight-mile safari trail. Of the preserve's six sections, four were inhabited by over a hundred lions living in prides and a herd of elephants on an island, while the other sections were occupied by zebras, giraffes, ostriches, white rhinoceroses, chimpanzees, and a dazzling array of other animals.

After completing my second undergrad year at Cornell University, I made the long drive down from New York and arrived in Florida for the job early in the summer of 1972. I couldn't have been more excited to have landed a three-month summer job there. Miraculously, I had gotten the job after writing a letter to the head ranger on a whim, and he subsequently interviewed me over the phone.

On my final approach to the safari park, I drove the one-mile stretch of road to the entrance, barely able to contain my enthusiasm as I passed signs like "People out of their cars will be eaten."

At the end of the road was a line of huts with palm-frond roofs and signs directing either to the left for the offices or to the right for the visitors' entrance. I followed the signs to the left, walked into the offices known by the employees as "Lion Base," and explained to the front desk staff who I was and why I was there. If I hadn't been sure about my decision before, the friendly greeting, the smell of the animals on the breeze, and the squawking of the African Gray parrot behind the desk reassured me that I had made the right choice.

I was escorted into a back office where a weather-beaten man dressed in safari clothes sat behind a desk. He introduced himself as Charles Durr, the park's head ranger with whom I had spoken earlier that year. We shook hands, and he introduced the man next to him as Bill McGrath, the assistant head ranger. Like Charles, Bill was dressed in a khaki safari outfit, but he was nowhere near as weathered as Charles. As they asked me about my drive from New York and began introducing me to the basics of the job, their casual style and their kind, easygoing attitudes put me at ease, and I immediately felt comfortable around my new coworkers.

As I took in my surroundings during the meeting, I was awed by the vast collection of wildlife books in Charles's office, and I couldn't help but admire the array of equipment he had on display. There was everything from walkie-talkies and firearms, to tranquilizing gear and an assortment of animal restraints, as well as a variety of medical instruments, much of which I had seen in books and on TV, but never dreamed I'd see, let alone handle, in real life.

The three of us briefly chatted. I asked to have two days to find a place to live for the summer, and then I'd be ready to work. As we finished talking, the radio on Charles's desk chattered out that some assistance was needed on Elephant Island.

"I'll go out to help," Bill told Charles. Then, turning to me, he said, "Mark, come along and I'll show you the park and how we work."

At this point, I was convinced I had died and gone to heaven. I was actually going to get up-close-and-personal with the animals on my first day! I also felt an immediate connection with Bill; he was easy to talk to, and I knew I was going to learn a great deal from him.

I followed Bill out the back door and into a zebra-striped Jeep. As he started the engine, Bill updated me on the plan: we were going to Section 5 to help a man named Mike secure the elephants for the night. I smiled and nodded as if I knew what he was talking about although, of course, I didn't. "Great!" I said, and I genuinely meant it, even though I had no clue what I was getting myself into.

We drove into the park through the front gate on a service road, passing by the cars that held visitors slowly entering the park. A twenty-foot-high fence towered on each side as we rumbled over a cattle guard (a shallow ditch with bars or slats across it that are spread far enough apart to keep hoof-stock from crossing over, but not people or vehicles). We had now entered Section 1, and, in my mind, it seemed like we had somehow been transported halfway around the world in the blink of an eye. I was suddenly surrounded on all sides by animals typically confined to an African savannah or the two-dimensional pages of a book. Giant elands, delicate gazelles, and scores of other herd-dwelling animals roamed freely just outside our vehicle.

We continued forward, and as we crossed the cattle guard entering into Section 2, Bill pointed to an elevated cabin on stilts about thirty feet above, and said, "That'll be your new home for the next while." I would be on assignment in the watchtower to look out for the safety of the park's visitors and animals.

The first thing that I realized about Section 2 was that instead of appearing like the plains we had just passed through in Section 1, this was lush with a vast variety of plants.

As we took the next turn, I was again in awe to see in person something I had only seen in books and movies. There, crossing the road right in front of us, was a majestic pride of lions. A very mature male lion was in the lead, followed by two beautiful lionesses, and lumbering after them were a number of cubs. Bill pointed out that the two females before me were the actual lionesses used in shooting the widely acclaimed movie *Born Free*.

As we waited for the lions to pass, Bill briefly checked in with the ranger on duty to care for the pride that day, and then we moved on.

"Mark, look over to your right," Bill said while pointing to a row of huts off to the side of the road. "Those huts are where the lions spend the night. Each evening they're rounded up, so they'll be in a safe place during the night."

Plus you'll know the other animals are safe from them! I thought with a half chuckle.

We continued moving forward and came to some thick hedgerows, very dense areas of foliage that were natural to the landscape and added to the scenery.

"See those hedgerows?" Bill asked.

"Yes, they're beautiful."

"Yes, they're beautiful to us, but I think that a lion must see them as the perfect hiding place. There's been many a night that the team and I have spent looking for a runaway lion hiding in those hedges after it's gotten away from the pride."

I wondered at both the dangers and excitement of such a task.

Before I could ask Bill about his hide-and-seek adventures with errant lions, my attention was commandeered at the sight of more prides of lions as we passed through Sections 3 and 4. Like the first pride I spotted, these were just as exciting. For me it's like seeing a sunset; it's never mundane.

We then arrived in Section 5, and for the nth time that day I saw something I could only have dreamt about seeing until that moment—a small herd of elephants roaming free on an island. We drove down a dirt road not meant for the public and came to a gate where a man leaning against a post was waiting for our arrival. It was Mike, the man who had called Lion Base asking for assistance.

We parked the Jeep, and Bill told me to wait in the vehicle as he was both safety-conscious and was unfamiliar with my skill set since I was new. He pointed out the dominant female, Donia, who was unusually large for an Asian pachyderm, as well as another Asian female elephant named Sabrina. He mentioned that if I ever had the chance to work with the elephants, I should be especially careful around Sabrina as she had recently put a very experienced ranger in the hospital when he got between her and a wall. Seeing the elephants this close and hearing his story, I had no problem waiting in the Jeep to observe.

Every evening the elephants were herded into a shelter for their protection overnight. This process required two people to do so safely, which is why Mike had called Lion Base for help. I watched as he gently guided the elephants into the barn by holding onto Donia's ear and letting her take the lead. Sabrina followed, and then all the other younger elephants went in with Bill bringing up the rear. The herd was secured for the night.

Over the coming weeks, every day I went to my job mindful that I was living my dream. The past two summer breaks I had worked on a thoroughbred horse farm in Ocala, Florida. Now I was learning and working with wildlife in an environment that was as nurturing to me as it was to the amazed visitors and magnificent animals in the park.

As a new employee, I did my time in the tower watching the daily scene of people and animals coming and going. This position tended to be incredibly tedious, so, to say the least, I was delighted when given opportunities to take on other responsibilities.

I was also fortunate to have found a lifelong friend in Bill, who, along with his wife Linda, kindly rented me a room for the summer. Linda also worked at Lion Country Safari with responsibilities for the petting zoo, the nursery, and the educational programs. As I was a pre-veterinary student, it was heaven for me to live and work with people who shared my love and passion for animals.

Six weeks into the job, like many other mornings, our communal home smelled of freshly brewed coffee and toast competing with the very distinct smell of the lion cub we were caring for. Over breakfast, Linda talked about the program she was going to present at the school where she was taking the lion cub to visit that day. I shared that I was looking forward to seeing my parents who were in town visiting from New York. They were planning to take me on a short vacation to the island of Nassau the next day, so I was excited.

By this time, I'd been lucky enough to be given a chance to assist Bill with some duties in the park. On this morning, we finished breakfast quickly so we could get to the park early. We were eager to see whether a waterbuck had given birth during the night. If so, that would mean walking the section she was in to find the new calf.

A waterbuck is a large antelope whose natural instinct in giving birth is to hide the calf so that predators won't find it during the daylight hours. Shortly after birth, the first milk that a waterbuck calf gets from its mother is referred to as colostrum. Browner than milk and excreted for only the first forty-eight to seventy-two hours after birth, colostrum from a healthy mother is loaded with antibodies, something a calf critically needs to fight diseases that can be fatal to them.

At Lion Country Safari, once a newborn calf was located, a physical exam and many tests were performed. One was a field blood test to ensure the newborn had absorbed the life-protecting antibodies in the colostrum. If an infant calf was located and had not been able to ingest colostrum within the first seventy-two hours, then it could be supplemented with frozen colostrum kept on hand for just such an occurrence. So it was important that we find the calf in its first few days of life to check its health status, administer its first vaccinations and medication for parasites, and ensure the newborn calf was nursing, and if not, provide the frozen colostrum substitute.

The drive to work ushered Bill and me through the perimeter of the Everglades, while on the radio the news debated the various possibilities and outcomes of the Watergate story, which was gripping the nation. Washington, DC, felt like a different world than the one I was living in.

We rode into Section 1 of the park and spotted the mother waterbuck. It was immediately obvious that she had dropped—or given birth to—the calf. It's referred to as "dropped" because with waterbucks, as is the case with most wild hoof-stock species, the mother gives birth standing up. The calf drops to the ground and stands up almost immediately, ensuring that both the mother and baby are standing as quickly as possible to be able to spot or escape predators at a moment's notice.

We knew that since the waterbuck had already calved before the sun was up, the chance of us finding the newborn on the first day in the seventy-five-acre field was very slim. The mother knew instinctively to hide the calf before the sun came up, and the calf knew not to move a muscle in its hiding place to avoid attracting the attention of predators. It usually took many people and many hours to find a new calf, especially in a field that also contained an assortment of other animals, including herds of wildebeest, black buck, ostriches, hornbills, and other assorted African plains animals, including one large Cape buffalo by the name of Ralph.

Having spotted the new mother, and knowing it would be better to search for the baby waterbuck in the evening hours, we headed into Lion Base to start the day's work. I followed my routine that morning and went to the locker room/gun room to find out what my assignment was for the day. I picked up my radio and a twelve-gauge shotgun that would ride in the gun rack in the Jeep I was assigned to. My responsibilities would include the care and feeding of animals in Section 6 and assisting the head elephant keeper as needed.

I was excited by this assignment because it meant I wasn't going to be bored stuck in a gate tower. Now I was responsible for Section 6, which came with having my own vehicle and the freedom to get work done on my own schedule, except if called upon to help the elephant keeper. It also meant that while caring for the needs of herds of giraffe, rhinoceros, gazelle, impala, kudu, one solitary hippopotamus, and a variety of birds, I would have the opportunity to watch the chimpanzees on Chimp Island, located in the middle of Section 6. The chimp troop had been involved in one of Jane Goodall's studies, and was cared for by a very experienced keeper, Terry Wolf. Watching the chimps as Terry tended to them was something I always loved to see.

"Come in, Bagel," the call came over the radio in my Jeep sometime around midmorning. My radio name was Bagel, which I'm sure had a lot to do with the fact that I was from New York and Jewish.

I answered the radio call; it was the elephant keeper, Mike. "Bagel, I need you to go out to Elephant Island in Section 5, pick up a feed pail, and bring it back up to the kitchen."

I replied, "10–4,"—radio code for "understood"—and drove my Jeep over to Elephant Island.

Along the way, I passed my coworker Fred, who was taking care of a pride of lions. The magnificent patriarch of the pride was Massif, a regal 550-pound male lion. Somehow Fred had developed a relationship with Massif such that he could feed the great cat while standing on the other side of his Jeep.

I waved to Fred and moved on. Soon I parked my Jeep, headed to the gate, and unlocked it, then walked across the bridge over to Elephant Island.

In walking onto the island, I was entering Donia's realm. As the herd's matriarch, anything that happened on the island was done strictly with her blessing.

I had learned the protocol for entering the space was to approach Donia and let her smell my feet. In this way, she could tell people apart and know who was in her home. After the olfactory "handshake," the next step would be to take her ear and let her walk with me to the hut that contained the food pail I had come to retrieve. This was a routine I had become familiar with.

However, on this morning, being young and impatient, I elected to pat Donia on the trunk and bypass the foot-smelling formalities by just verbally mentioning what I was there to do as I flippantly walked away from her.

Only I didn't walk away, I flew!

With a single swipe of her massive trunk, Donia launched me into the air like a rag doll. I had been deemed a hostile intruder, or perhaps just someone with no manners, but whatever her reasoning, I quickly found myself flat on my back, Donia's weight slowly crushing me to death.

With no time to think, I instinctively went back to my training. I knew the only way to get her attention was to poke her in the eye, so, after desperately feeling around her face, I found an eye socket and jabbed as if my life depended on it. Which it did.

For an instant, the grande dame lifted her head, and I quickly seized the moment to roll off the island into the surrounding canal.

Once I was no longer on the island or in her domain, Donia no longer saw me as a threat; in her mind, the problem was solved, and she retreated.

One could argue that I went from a bad situation to worse, because alligators populated the canal. In reality, alligators will generally run away from humans versus attacking, even a human who's been trampled by an elephant. (Had the gators instead been their cousins the crocodiles, this story would have been the last one of my young life.) Still, it's not a place I'd suggest going for a swim.

I must have been in shock as I floated there in the canal, because neither Donia's presence twenty feet in front of me nor the injuries I sustained kept me from laughing hysterically. I laughed and laughed as my arm spun round, clearly broken, and for reasons unknown, I thought of my kindergarten teacher, Ms. Bevin.

I had been so nervous when I started going to school every day that I frequently became nauseated on the bus ride there. With a kind heart and a strong stomach, Ms. Bevin took to meeting me at the bus with a bag for me to throw up in, much like a flight attendant with an airsick bag.

Perhaps Ms. Bevin's seemingly random appearance from the depths of my memory was a way of comforting myself in a time of trauma. Whatever the reason, thoughts of her kept me company as I continued laughing in the canal.

Eventually, I heard a vehicle's quick stop, and then Fred appeared at my side. While tending to Massif and his lion pride some two hundred yards away, Fred had seen Donia fling me, then came flying across the field in his Jeep to assist.

Fred quickly but carefully helped me out of the canal and into the Jeep, then secured the island and radioed Lion Base that I was injured and he was bringing me in. Even after we made it to Lion Base and the ambulance arrived to take me to the hospital, I was still laughing.

I know some aspects of shock can be harmful and other aspects numb a person. The numbing aspect wore off in the ambulance as I headed towards Good Samaritan Hospital in West Palm Beach—that's when the pain set in. At the same time, the realization that I had almost died hit me as well, almost as powerfully as Donia had just a short time before.

Maybe it's adrenaline or all the other related chemicals that are released when your body goes into shock, or maybe it was just my genetic makeup, but I willed myself to remain conscious and not give in to the pain until I reached the hospital. I knew I needed to be the one to tell my parents what was happening. My parents needed to hear it from me, especially my loving, traditional, Jewish mom. They needed to hear my voice. And perhaps I needed to hear theirs as well.

In the emergency room, I pleaded with the doctor to let me be the one to call my parents, and he finally gave in and handed me the phone.

"Dad," I said very calmly, "I don't think we're going to be able to go on vacation."

"Why not?"

"Because I almost got killed by an elephant," I mustered the answer. "But I'm okay. Let me have the doctor explain."

I handed the phone to the physician then proceeded to be in and out of consciousness for the next two-and-a-half days.

In my semiconscious state at that time, my parents were by my side, for which I was very grateful. But I was also quite aware of different people lifting my side up and marveling at my back. It wasn't until about four days later when I was fully conscious, that I found out that in addition to two broken bones in my forearm an assortment of other animals, including herds of wildebeest, black buck, ostriches, hornbills, and other assorted African plains animals, including one large Cape buffalo by the name of Ralph.

Having spotted the new mother, and knowing it would be better to search for the baby waterbuck in the evening hours, we headed into Lion Base to start the day's work. I followed my routine that morning and went to the locker room/gun room to find out what my assignment was for the day. I picked up my radio and a twelve-gauge shotgun that would ride in the gun rack in the Jeep I was assigned to. My responsibilities would include the care and feeding of animals in Section 6 and assisting the head elephant keeper as needed.

I was excited by this assignment because it meant I wasn't going to be bored stuck in a gate tower. Now I was responsible for Section 6, which came with having my own vehicle and the freedom to get work done on my own schedule, except if called upon to help the elephant keeper. It also meant that while caring for the needs of herds of giraffe, rhinoceros, gazelle, impala, kudu, one solitary hippopotamus, and a variety of birds, I would have the opportunity to watch the chimpanzees on Chimp Island, located in the middle of Section 6. The chimp troop had been involved in one of Jane Goodall's studies, and was cared for by a very experienced keeper, Terry Wolf. Watching the chimps as Terry tended to them was something I always loved to see.

"Come in, Bagel," the call came over the radio in my Jeep sometime around midmorning. My radio name was Bagel, which I'm sure had a lot to do with the fact that I was from New York and Jewish.

I answered the radio call; it was the elephant keeper, M
"Bagel, I need you to go out to Elephant Island in Section 5
up a feed pail, and bring it back up to the kitchen."

role in protecting her herd. In doing so, she taught me two lessons I would remember the rest of my life: never take an animal for granted, and following the rules can have tremendous value.

As I've recently revisited the incident in its retelling, I've come to realize that although it almost ended my life, it was a moment that confirmed that my decision to be a veterinarian was, in fact, my life's calling.

Even after my harrowing encounter, I still had a lot to learn. One morning at Lion Country Safari, just weeks after the Donia incident, I decided to relieve my boredom from manning the gate in the tower by getting a close-up photograph of Ralph, the resident Cape buffalo. Still afflicted with delusions of invulnerability, I thought that I could capture that image safely from one side of a manmade termite mound near the gate while Ralph was standing just on the other side. I had a modest Kodak Instamatic, which meant I'd have to be *very* close to get a good shot from just a few feet away. I moved in and successfully snapped the picture, a fully framed face of an 1,100 pound Cape buffalo.

I didn't realize at the time how dangerous this was. Cape buffalo are second only to hippopotami when it comes to violent deaths to humans by mammals in Africa. Unfortunately, they were just as deadly at Lion Country Safari. Two years after taking this photo I learned that, near the same termite mound, Ralph had killed Malcolm, an experienced park ranger I knew and from whom I had learned a lot while working at the park.

Chapter 2

THOROUGHBREDS

 **Our lives can take unforeseen twists** and turns, led by seemingly random connections and the choices we make, which can in turn lead to new opportunities and lifelong lessons that set us on a course for a career. Such was the case when I was in high school, five years before my untoward interaction with Donia, when I went looking for summer employment. Having swept floors in a butcher shop in my previous job, for my next position I wanted something different from the typical teenage jobs of waiting tables, working retail, or serving up fast food. I thought about trying to get work at the local veterinarian's office, but there were a dozen other kids lined up for that. Instead, I made my way around to the horse stables in the area and looked for employment.

I grew up in Hicksville, New York. The town was on Long Island, just thirty miles from the hustle of Manhattan. Even though it was a suburb of the City, equestrian centers could be found in nearby villages—reminiscent of a time before World War II when this bustling area of 50,000 residents consisted of nothing more than pastoral rural farms.

I must have applied to more than a dozen stables that summer, but, one by one, each stable turned me down. That was, of course, until I met Mr. Peterson. At every other place I had applied, I'd been introduced to the stable manager when I asked about a job, but luckily when I came by New Market Horse Farm that day, I instead met the owner, Mr. Jack Peterson. I talked to him for a while and then said, "I've set my goals on being a veterinarian, and you can depend on me."

"Okay Mark," Mr. Peterson responded, "If you can show up next Saturday, you've got a job."

From that Saturday in 1967 on through my high school graduation in 1970, my mom would give me a ride to the stables. I'd go to work every Saturday and Sunday and start the day mucking stalls—a waste-cleaning job exponentially more voluminous than picking up after a dog—followed by an afternoon spent bathing, grooming, and cooling down the horses after others had ridden them. Occasionally, I had the opportunity to exercise horses for wealthy owners who couldn't be there to hone their equestrian dressage skills or play polo on the nearby fields. Most of the time it was hard work, but I loved every minute of it because I was learning about horses. Plus, by the end, I could handle a wheelbarrow better than most anyone.

Since my job at the stable was weekends only, when I graduated high school and before heading off to college at Cornell, I sought out additional work to supplement my bank account. Not far from my home, my Uncle Al owned a factory that produced plastic bags. He generously offered me a job as an assembly-line worker. For my age and lack of experience it paid well. Little did I know it would teach me a lifelong lesson. After two weeks, I quickly realized I was craving to expand my knowledge of working with animals and that factory work, even though it paid well, was not fulfilling to me. I distinctly remember promising myself that

I would make sure I excelled at Cornell so that I would be able to attain my dream of being a veterinarian.

I shared with my parents how much I thirsted for the opportunity to work in some field that was related to my passion. At the time, my dad worked for a large manufacturer of women's dresses and knew the owner of the company, Philip Iselin, who was also an owner and president of the New York Jets. Beyond his interests in professional football, Mr. Iselin also had a passion for horseracing and was president of the Monmouth Park Jockey Club in Oceanport as well as director of the Thoroughbred Racing Association.

My dad talked to Mr. Iselin about my desire to be a veterinarian and my experience working in the riding stables. In turn, Mr. Iselin spoke to a Mr. Savin about my going down to work on his horse farm in Florida. And by some miracle, soon after that and only three weeks after my graduation from Hicksville High School, my dad and I made a road trip a thousand miles south along the eastern seaboard to Ocala, Florida, where I would live and work at the farm on my own.

Winding our way through progressive changes in topography, climate, and culture, we eventually reached our destination some seventy miles northwest of Orlando. It was a land of beautiful forests, rivers, and rolling farmland.

This was 1970 and segregation was a way of life. My first graphic exposure to this was driving through the town with my dad. I saw streets paved with asphalt in the "white" part of town and when we transitioned into the "black" part of town, the streets were dirt. It dawned on me that this adventure was going to be more than just about working with animals but a submersion into a different culture from my sheltered upbringing in New York.

This was even more apparent to me when I got to know the people I worked with; the farm employed only white people. I did not realize then, but looking back it prepared me to understand and develop the skills to be sensitive and able to work, listen, and learn from people who had different values and lived their lives differently, without compromising my beliefs. These skills are imperative for a doctor to be successful in a diverse world.

It was my first time away from home and I was solely dependent on myself. I lived alone in a trailer and quickly came to appreciate my mother's hard work and her preparation of hot meals at the dinner table every night growing up. Now living in Ocala, if I didn't fix my own dinner, I didn't eat.

I also quickly received a crash course in the expectations of Southern formality from my new boss, Mr. Pat Hunter, the man in charge of the farm. Upon giving me a directive to do a task, I had responded with a casual, "Yeah," to which he immediately informed me, "Son, down here we say, 'Yes sir' and 'No sir.'"

Although still just seventeen years old, my experience working at the riding stables back in New York made me think I knew it all. So I was dismayed when, for the first week, I was relegated to washing walls in the barn with little discussion other than a "Yes sir!" I had come here to learn about animals, and yet I wasn't even being trusted with mucking out the stables.

One day, I was at my usual dull routine when I heard a man calling out, "Whoa! Whoa boy!" I came out of the barn to see what the commotion was all about, and just ahead of me I saw a thousand pounds of thoroughbred stallion going off like a powder keg, kicking and rearing. He dwarfed the six-foot, four-inch, towering figure of a man who was trying to calm him down. The fiery, raging stallion about to explode was unlike any horse I'd ever seen before.

As I watched the tense spectacle, I suddenly understood this was another league altogether. Aisco Farm was home to the

Olympic athletes of thoroughbred horseracing.

Although lighter in weight than the average horse, thorough-breds are immensely powerful and immaculately bred for brilliant bursts of speed. Aisco had the best of breed on their 580-acre farm, ample room to raise horses and even a herd of cattle. Stakes winners at Monmouth Park, Saratoga, and Belmont Park, horses in Aisco's stable would in the coming years go on to race against Secretariat in the Kentucky Derby and beget one of the most winning legacies in thoroughbred racing history through the descendants of a horse named Mr. Prospector. At the end of their lives, Secretariat and Mr. Prospector were buried next to each other at Claireborn Farm in Paris, Kentucky, where they both lived out their final years.

I was too young to fully appreciate the hallowed ground on which I was standing; I just knew as I watched the stallion rearing and kicking that I was the most frightened, or rather awestruck, I had ever been around an animal.

I had learned from my days at the riding stables to be careful when around horses. There are routines and protocols to follow, such as approaching and mounting a horse only from the left side. In addition, there is particular body language to watch for that can signal a horse's mood, such as its ears pinned back or a hind hoof cocked and ready. A horse will sometimes react suddenly to anything from a loud backfire to the soft landing of a horsefly, so it is crucial to remain mindful to signs of danger because it can literally make the difference between life and death. I would learn years later that the most likely animal to seriously hurt or even kill a veterinarian is a horse. Some of that has to do with the often-repeated falsehood from backyard horse owners who say, "My horse never kicks or bites." But you only have to work around horses for a short time to learn that *every* horse can kick and bite.

"Whoa, whoa!" I heard the man say again as he calmly quieted the horse. His name was Charles Hunter, and he was the nephew of the man who ran Aisco. Just moments before, an unknown something had spooked the high-strung steed as Charles led him down a path, and in a split second the stallion was worked up into a frenzy. This was a very muscular male thoroughbred driven by a potentially deadly combination of extra testosterone and adrenaline.

Because of a stallion's colossal power and unpredictable nature, equestrians employ techniques that make the horse assume the person is the one in control, such as threading the chain on the end of the lead over its nose to get its attention. But anyone who has worked around horses long enough knows that it's a delusion to think you're *actually* in charge. You can never forget that, in reality, the horse is much more powerful, and the real trick is getting it to believe *you're* the one in the lead. On this day, that was fortunately the case as Charles expertly avoided flying hooves and stomping legs, skillfully convincing this thoroughbred stud to walk like a gentleman.

In that same moment, my attitude about "only washing walls" also settled down as I realized I still had a lot to learn. I not only gained a newfound respect for the power of magnificent racehorses but also for the people who worked with and handled them on a daily basis. Some farmhands may not have been extensively educated in the sense of traditional schooling, yet they had an enormous wealth of knowledge about animals. So even though I would soon be starting school at Cornell in the fall as a pre-veterinary student, I knew I didn't need to wait to be in college to start learning.

I dug into my chores and earned my way past the "hazing" phase of my first weeks on the farm. I worked six long days a week to earn my $75 weekly salary and was launched into manhood with a routine of hard work that started at 6:00 AM sharp—not 6:05 AM—every morning. As an adult, I was expected to follow the tractor as it pulled the hay baler while hoisting seventy-five-pound hay bales up onto a trailer bed. As the trailer filled up, that meant not only lifting but then throwing the bale as high as ten feet off the ground. I was treated like every other farmhand and expected to keep up with the others in the most physically demanding job of my life.

The sting of early mornings and hard work was taken away by the beautiful sight of impressive horses in pastures kissed by dawning sunlight. With dewy green grass and the perfect brown fences, it looked like something out of a Budweiser commercial. I not only survived the summer working on the farm, I loved it. Even though my nickname was Yankee, I guess I earned the respect of Mr. Hunter, as he invited me back to work on the farm the following summer. I was even offered a coveted mobile home on the farm. My trailer sat right next to the yearlings' barn, a pristine circular building that the owner, Mr. Abraham Savin, designed around a stately giant oak tree. Featured in the inner atrium of the building, it served as the epicenter of his horse farm.

I was now trusted to work with broodmares, their foals and yearlings. Each morning, I would walk the horses out of the barn and release them to their respective paddocks. I learned the value of taking the time to observe animals. By carefully watching each horse during this daily morning routine, over time, I came to know each animal's demeanor, habits, and body language. If a horse didn't run along the fence, vocalize, or exhibit their other usual behaviors, I'd report back that something seemed off or didn't look the same.

By starting at the bottom, literally in the muck, I learned

critical knowledge for someone who wants to be a vet, like: what does a healthy stool look like? I learned about an animal's normal and, on occasion, abnormal physiological habits. People think animals can't talk, but when you learn to observe indicators such as their eyes and ears and postures, you learn to "hear" them. I was taught to be careful about small but meaningful signals and behaviors, like not having a handkerchief or towels flapping around—things that might spook or set them off. By doing my part in being observant and mindful of such things, I could make the animals' lives better, as well as improve my chances for staying safe or being able to predict trouble.

On my days off, I would spend time with veterinarians in the area. Dr. Reuben Brawner was a veterinary pioneer and cornerstone of the Florida horse industry. Dr. Brawner generously took me under his wing, letting me tag along on his rounds to the neighboring horse farms. He was always very thorough and professional, and I was thrilled to be able to assist him.

One day, he examined one of the most beautiful horses I'd ever seen who, as it turned out, was also considered to be one of the greatest racehorses of all time: Dr. Fegor, named in honor of the neurosurgeon who saved the owner's life after he suffered a serious fall from horseback. Dr. Fegor is still the only horse to have ever held four titles in a single racing season: champion handicap horse, champion sprinter, and co-champion grass horse—all won in 1968, when he was also named Horse of the Year. I felt it a great honor to hold this magnificent animal as Dr. Brawner examined him.

Another veterinarian who generously let me tag along with him as he made his rounds was Dr. Earl Schobert, the first vet to work at Busch Gardens, a popular tourist attraction featuring seventy acres of the "Serengeti Plain," at the time the largest free-roaming enclosed habitat for exotic animals outside of Africa. I would drive to Tampa excited to see all the varied species of animals in the park and spend the day with Dr. Schubert as he tended to them.

Dr. Brawner and Dr. Schobert were not only veterinary pioneers in their respective fields of expertise but also true animal lovers, always willing to go above and beyond to help any animal that came their way. Both men served as a source of inspiration to me as an eager young student, treating their human clients with the same respect and care they afforded their patients. For me, it was the beginning of recognizing and understanding the human-animal bond.

For two summers, I worked at Aisco Farm among the elite of thoroughbred foals, yearlings, and studs. I came home to New York each fall like a young man back from military boot camp, changed and more independent. Not only had I learned more about animals on a world-class horse farm, but I had also gained a greater appreciation for the power of thoroughbred horses and a respect and deeper understanding of the value of observation in working with them and their unpredictable nature.

An added bonus was that I had not only survived but thrived living independently, and in a different culture. Looking back, this experience was the first time I saw the role that the human-animal bond played in bringing people of very different backgrounds together. Little did I know then the amazing journey that was just beginning for me.

*The beginning of a wonderful career for both
me and a foal on Aisco Farm!*

Chapter 3

GUS

During four summers while off from my studies at Cornell I worked at Lion Country Safari; two in Florida and then two at the company's sister park in Grand Prairie, Texas, located between Fort Worth and Dallas. Working with large, exotic animals taught me many things, including the biggest lesson—having respect for them, which came from Donia when I failed to follow the rules.

It was in Texas that I received my most powerful lesson in the unpredictability of animals. This lesson was delivered by a rhinoceros named Gus and in the most unexpected way imaginable.

Gus was a fully mature white rhinoceros. Actually, a white rhinoceros isn't white. The animal gets its name because it has a wide mouth differentiating it from a black rhinoceros that has a very pointed, prehensile mouth. It was the Dutch who first named the white rhinoceros using the Dutch word *wijd*, which means wide but sounds like white.

Gus was 6,000 pounds of armored muscle—more than a small SUV—and had a three-and-a-half-foot horn protruding from his nose. He was roughly the size of eight horses, enormous even for a rhinoceros, and he ruled the section of the park he lived in. He wasn't an aggressive or dangerous animal, but you would have to be foolish to disregard a living tank, especially one who just a week before had pushed a farm truck weighing in at more than 8,000 pounds sideways into a lake because it was in his way. The truck was totaled. Gus was completely unharmed.

On this particular day, I was part of a four-man team helping the park's veterinarian, Dr. Joe Cannon, do routine physical exams, and one of the animals to check was Gus.

By this time each member of the team was familiar with the routine. The physical exam would include making various measurements of Gus's horn and other parts of his body. Taking Gus's vital signs included drawing a blood sample from the vein in his ear and taking a rectal temperature.

As you might imagine, you don't just walk up to a rhinoceros and ask him to lift his tail so you can insert a thermometer. To do this safely, we would have to completely immobilize Gus by administering a tranquilizer. In this case, the drug of choice was called Etorphine, also known as M99, a powerful opioid derivative a thousand times more potent than morphine, strictly used for purposes of temporarily immobilizing large animals.

M99 is so concentrated that it only takes a small amount to tranquilize an animal successfully. It's so potent that a single drop absorbed by a grown human adult can kill—and it has.

At the same time, we also carried a dose of Diprenorphine, also known as M50/50, which can reverse the effects of M99. For the well-being of a tranquilized animal, being able to reverse the immobilization effects quickly is necessary for the animal, both physiologically and in its ability to protect itself.

First we shot Gus with a dart filled with the appropriate dose of M99. The signs that M99 is working are quite evident because the animal develops a uniquely distinct walk. The animal will start to prance, lifting its legs up as if to stand on its toes. The animal sometimes runs around erratically preceding this unique gait.

In a rhinoceros, you often see the unique gait without the erratic running, and then it quietly and easily lies down on its sternum and rests its head on the ground. We expected to see this reaction from Gus, and that's precisely what he did fifteen minutes after being struck by the dart.

Once Gus was lying down, our team exited the vehicle quickly but quietly; he might still have been sensitive to sound, and we didn't want to excite him. We also wanted to work as efficiently and quickly as possible, then reverse the M99 with M50/50 to get the animal back on its feet.

With Gus now lying quietly on the ground, the four of us surrounded the immense rhino and went to work. One person covered his eyes with a towel to keep him calm while maintaining a close watch to make sure he could breathe easily. Another took various measurements of his horn and overall body length to put into his medical file. Dr. Cannon listened to his heart and then was about to take blood from his ear vein.

One of my responsibilities was to take Gus's temperature using a rectal thermometer, which I inserted appropriately, and the other was to remove the dart from where it had entered his hindquarters.

The dart used to immobilize Gus was specially designed, with M99 in the front chamber and a gunpowder charge in the back. When the dart enters the skin after being fired from an air rifle, the charge in the back chamber explodes, pressing the plunger forward and delivering the injection of the tranquilizer.

When a keeper removes the dart, the standard procedure is to shake it to confirm that all of the M99 had been injected. You know it's empty when you shake it because the dart's inner chamber, now being empty, allows the plunger to go back and forth creating a very distinct clicking noise.

As usual, I removed the dart according to protocol and shook it. However, to my shock, it didn't make the expected clicking noise. In fact, it made no noise whatsoever. My mind was racing, wondering how this could be the case. At the same time my hand could tell by the weight of the dart that my greatest fear was confirmed. The dart was still fully loaded. Upon entering Gus's body, the dart never fired, and in fact, he received no M99.

The reality hit me like a freight train. Gus was allowing us to do our work while *fully awake!*

Operating in a strange fog of disbelief and utter amazement, I needed to immediately inform our team without alarming the otherwise compliant rhinoceros. Suppressing my desire to scream, I gave a muffled shout to Dr. Cannon—in a voice two octaves higher than I usually spoke. "The dart didn't fire! Gus is awake!"

The others, all experienced park rangers, realized the seriousness of the situation.

For all the training and experience we each had, none of us had been able to detect Gus's dance performance. With no ability to predict what might happen next, we went about business as usual.

With measured and steady breathing, I removed the rectal thermometer. One would assume that *inserting* the thermometer would have bothered Gus, but that indignity hadn't fazed him. When I removed it, however, he opened his eye! Then he snorted and started to rise.

To this day, I wonder if reinserting the thermometer would have settled him down again. I have yet to find anyone volunteering to run a study on whether the insertion of a glass rod into the rectum of a fully conscious rhino will make him calm, so I suppose we'll never know.

As soon as we finished, we gathered our equipment and raced to the truck faster than I've ever seen four people move. Once safely loaded inside, we sighed and counted our blessings.

Confirming my suspicions, Gus hadn't received even a single drop of anesthesia, yet he had been polite enough to allow us to do all that work on him. Our guess was that when he was shot with the dart, he was so used to the usual dance that he simply assumed the role. In an Academy Award–winning performance, he went through the usual steps from his memory.

I realize how fortunate my colleagues and I were to have been through this experience with no adverse outcome. I am privileged that the powerful and amazing Gus taught me another invaluable lesson. Animals are unpredictable, and we should always have the utmost respect for them.

Chapter 4

ISRAEL

In the pitch black of night, I heard a distinct metallic *click,* followed by a man's voice authoritatively whispering, *"Shalom, mah sheem-khah?"*

I turned to my left and found myself looking down the wrong end of a rifle! Never before had I experienced a gun threateningly aimed at my face. The barrel seemed as long as the Lincoln Tunnel, and it was all I could see as my senses were heightened and focused on that and only that. It felt like an eternity has passed—*almost* enough time for my biological systems to evacuate, but I was saved that embarrassment when the man turned on and aimed a small pencil light at me, blinding me.

"Mah sheem-khah?" the male voice quietly insisted again.

I spoke very little Hebrew, and at the moment I wasn't sure I could even speak English, but it finally registered in my mind that he was asking for my name. So, finally, my words did come out and I explained who I was and what I was there for.

The man on the other end of the firearm appeared to check a clipboard. His face was covered, and because of the glaring light I couldn't see him very well or read his face, but then I saw him lower the gun and he said, in a very kind, singsong voice, "Shalom Dr. Goldstein. Do you know where you're going?"

Emotionally drained but relieved beyond belief, I weakly answered, "Yes."

Paradoxically, I was lucky to find myself at the end of this gun barrel. I was living and working in Israel during the summer between my third and fourth years of vet school. At school, I had gotten to know Dr. Pinni Rippin, an Israeli veterinarian who was teaching for a year at the College of Veterinary Medicine at Cornell as a visiting professor. Near the end of the spring term, he surprised me with an offer to stay with his family during the summer. Dr. Rippin arranged for me to work with a veterinarian in Israel, Dr. Rami Arbeitman, while Dr. Rippin was still in the United States. I jumped at the opportunity.

One of many reasons I chose to be a veterinarian was I knew I could go anywhere in the world and find purpose and a commonality of professional thinking. Being a veterinarian is a global profession; there is no continent or country without animals. Also, being Jewish, I was excited to travel to Israel and see the historic sites and experience my family's cultural heritage.

The Rippin family home was in Afula, a small traditional town and regional hub of the spacious and fertile Jezreel Valley. In ancient times, the Jezreel Valley had been host to great turmoil, but in 1977 it was a peaceful setting of land tilled into a beautiful patchwork of vast open fields and small ribbon gardens. A short distance north of Afula was the town of Nazareth. From its perch atop a high mountain ridge, one of the most picturesque scenes in the country was the pastoral landscape of the basin below.

Many inhabitants of the Jezreel Valley were immigrants who came to the area with hopes of building a better life. They settled in agricultural villages known either as a *kibbutz,* a farming enclave where the land was communally owned and worked, or a *moshav,* where the people lived and worked communally but the property was held independently.

Such communities were first established in the early twentieth century as part of the Zionist movement. Over the decades, the population had grown as wars and conflicts rearranged the boundaries of nations, and people from afar and with varying backgrounds poured in.

Growing up in the New York City area, I was familiar with living in an ethnic melting pot, but this region of the world, with its unique mélange of people and cultures, was a different experience altogether. The world was much more complex than the small universe in which I had grown up, and my experience with the gun-toting guard was a stark reminder of that.

"Dr. Goldstein," the rifleman smiled, "you can proceed, but you must go no faster than twenty-five miles per hour and drive with no lights on."

I had been asked to come to moshav Tel Adashim, located between Afula and Nazareth, to teach a local veterinarian the method I had learned at Cornell to spay a dog. For my teaching assignment, I was to show up after dinner one evening at the vet's home.

A few days before the appointment, I was informed that the moshav was on alert to expect a "mock terrorist attack" in the next three days, a sort of fire drill for the whole village. To avoid someone confusing the drill with a real attack, the community had been given notice of the upcoming exercise.

In turning down the road to the moshav, I knew the drill must be underway because the whole area was pitch black. It seemed the village had simply disappeared, much like the mythical town in the musical *Brigadoon*, in which a town shows up only one day every hundred years and then vanishes for another century.

Tel Adashim, did not disappear, however, but was hiding under a cloak of darkness.

Traversing a village under mock attack in the dark was certainly not something I had ever experienced back in Hicksville, New York, but I kept my composure. I soon found the veterinarian's house, parked, then quietly made my way to the front door and lightly knocked. A moment later, someone silently and slightly opened the door, whisked me inside, and quickly closed the door behind me.

It was completely dark inside, but once the door was completely closed, a light was turned on in the kitchen. As my eyes adjusted to the brightness, I looked around the room. Blackout curtains hung on all the windows to block light from emanating to the outside world instead of the usual task of keeping sunlight from pouring in. In the middle of the room was a makeshift surgery table and all the required equipment, surrounded by two veterinarians and the home's family members, all coming together in a make-do but very properly outfitted "surgical" kitchen.

It was a somewhat surreal scene, but everyone proceeded as if this was all very normal. Following suit, in a very uneventful fashion, I performed the surgeries, successfully spaying one female dog and castrating one male dog. Just as we finished, the lights throughout the house turned on. Apparently, the terrorist exercise was completed as well.

I said my goodbyes and walked out the front door to see the moshav had magically returned. My reality returned to a distant land of beauty and people that in some surreal way felt like an extension of my own home.

For the most part, my days in Afula were not nearly as dramatic as this event but fascinating nonetheless. We started at 6:00 AM in order to avoid the heat of the hot summer. Dr. Arbeitman picked me up every morning to begin a day of visiting the nearby towns and farms where we would tend to agricultural stock—mainly cows, sheep, and goats, or the occasional horse. Sometimes, townspeople sought our opinion about the dogs and cats that inhabited the farms as well. At midday, we'd enjoy a big meal for lunch and then, as is the custom in most traditional cultures from hot climates, take a couple of hours off for a nap before working the remainder of the afternoon to complete the day.

Dr. Arbeitman's typical visit for routine veterinary care involved going down a row of cows, which were lined up for me to run tests for tuberculosis (TB) or do pregnancy checks. Determining if a female cow was pregnant was nothing like the method for humans—testing with a urine sample. The procedure required that I put on a long plastic glove, up to my shoulder, so I could perform a physical examination known as "rectal palpation," or "preg-checking." The glove was well lubricated to allow for easier insertion of my arm into the cow's rectum in order to feel the bovine reproductive organs. An experienced veterinarian can diagnose within a matter of seconds whether the female is pregnant or determine the stage of estrous the cow is cycling through by the shape and feel of the ovaries, uterine horns or fallopian tubes, and the uterus.

As I went along taking notes on the findings of my examinations, a farmhand held each animal. Often, these workers spoke little to no English or had no formal education. Many were Arabs or Jewish European immigrants speaking various languages. Remarkably, any differences between them would dissipate as the universal language of animal care transcended any tiffs, with everyone working side by side, as a team.

My idealistic views were juxtaposed against other jolting realities that often unexpectedly punctuated my experience. During one of my midday siesta slumbers, I was awakened by a loud noise. I looked out the window above my bed to see a tank battalion rumbling by, a not-so-subtle reminder that I wasn't at home anymore but living in a region of ongoing conflicts. Another time, I worked with a farmer in the Golan Heights. He held his cow with one hand and grasped an automatic weapon with the other, but as I came to learn he had good reason to do so. This area is northeast of Afula, past the Sea of Galilee, also known as Lake Kinneret. The Golan overlooks the Hula Valley, Israel's richest agricultural area. The plateau was also home to former Syrian artillery embankments used in decades past to rain down death on the plains below. The territory was acquired in 1967, when the Six-Day War ended such showers of terror, yet tension in the area persisted, hence the farmer's choice of "tools."

Another early morning, I was visiting a beautiful, well-kept dairy barn not far from Afula. As I was getting equipment from the truck to do routine TB testing on a herd of cattle, I heard an unfamiliar mechanical noise coming from over a tall hedgerow. Curious, I climbed up on a nearby tractor to see over the hedge. To my surprise, sitting in the middle of the next field was a fighter jet with its engines running. As I reached for my camera to take a picture, a gruff, authoritative voice commanded, "Get down now!" I turned to see the dairy farmer aiming a pitchfork at me. I had no doubt he meant business if I didn't comply immediately, so I quickly retreated.

When I was a child, for eight years I went to Hebrew school. Two evenings a week and on Sundays, I learned about the ancient and modern history of Israel. During the weekdays in secular school, I studied history lessons mainly focused on the history of the United States, an overview of immigrant peoples from other lands, and the events of recent centuries. In America, the native populations and their way of life, ones that had been on the continent for thousands of years before the influx of Europeans, were in many ways lost, like footnote ghosts of the past, not only in books but in fact. But in Israel, the ancient and rich heritage I had learned about was preserved. Experiencing places that I had studied, knowing that I might be walking in the footsteps that my ancestors had many millennia earlier, brought tears to my eyes.

I was exposed to many experiences far beyond textbook learning. While traveling on a seven-day tour in the Sinai Desert near the Red Sea, I got a lesson in time-honored animal practices from a modern Bedouin at the base of Mount Sinai.

Earlier that day, I had climbed to the summit of the mountain. I have never been in a place more spiritual than when I stood on the crest of Mount Sinai. On the same ground where Moses stood while the tribes of Israel, recently freed from slavery, awaited his descent to the base of the mountain, I felt I should be pure in thought and action.

After I descended the trail, an Israeli soldier who was my guide for the trip, introduced me to a man dressed in traditional garb from head to toe, adding to my sense of awe that day. His long, flowing robes and head cloth revealed only his face and hands, notably weathered from the harsh elements. From my previous interactions with other people from his culture, I recognized him as a Bedouin.

The Bedouin people were peaceful nomadic societies inhabiting the region for thousands of years, herding sheep, goats, and camels as a way of life. This man's entire world was the surrounding fifty miles, a barren desert that blistered in the summer with daytime temperatures of 130°F before dropping to just above freezing at night. He had been born and would likely die within that radius.

The man's name I have long forgotten, but not his actions. "Mark," my guide said, "We have been invited to join this man for dinner."

I couldn't even imagine where the fire and water would come from, let alone the food, but said, "Please give him my thanks," as I smiled in the Bedouin's direction.

"I explained to him that you are educated in veterinary medicine," the guide continued. "He has also invited you to observe the dinner preparations." My interest was piqued, so I nodded my head in acceptance of his invitation.

The Bedouin began preparations for the meal by gathering remnants of plants and shrubs and using my lighter to start a fire. Periodically, he would disappear behind rocks, or go over to a large sack hanging from a tree, and return with spices or handmade utensils and pots. Using our water cans, he filled the pots and set them over the fire. Then, as if from a magician's hat, a goat appeared. Two other Bedouin men had brought the animal there, and I hadn't even seen them

I had a sizable pocketknife with me, one that I'd carried on camping trips in my childhood. I offered it to him to use in preparing the meal. He gratefully took the knife, admiring the sharpness of the blade.

Back at home, fending for a meal meant going to the corner grocery store, where a cornucopia of food was available, from brightly colored fruits and vegetables to cuts of meat butchered by people in white coats and neatly packaged for sale under plastic wrap in refrigerated cases. There was no grocery store in this corner of the Sinai, no neatly packaged anything. But contrary to my modern senses, the desert still provided.

As the Bedouin prepared the goat for dinner, I watched in total amazement as he used techniques and methods passed on from generation to generation, probably for millennia. After a humane death, he carefully inspected every part of the animal to make sure it was healthy to eat. It looked like he had been taught how to do a formal necropsy, the animal-equivalent term of an autopsy done on a person. The way he examined, cleaned, and handled the meat would have passed a modern-day health inspection.

Further, I also noted that every part of the animal was to be used in some manner, with everything put into pails. From eyeballs to intestines to brains, there was no waste. I realized that not only was I learning ways to exist in an unforgiving environment, but he was also teaching me universal methods in practical animal care and living. At the same time, I could see in his eyes and actions that he respected my knowledge and willingness to learn.

As the sun set over the western horizon, other members of his family appeared, again seemingly from nowhere. We all enjoyed a feast fit for a king, in a place where it would've taken me all day just to figure out how to boil water.

At the end of the night, he returned my clean pocketknife, exhibiting great care and thanks for sharing it. We parted with me wishing him, *"As-Salaam-Alaikum,"* and he wishing me, *"Shalom,"* each bidding one another, "Peace be upon you," in the other's language.

That night we slept at the site. When I awoke the next morning, the Bedouins were nowhere to be seen. From our short encounter, I realized these resourceful people had not only learned to live in the desert but thrive.

That summer of living in a setting of vastly different cultures and challenging environments was a powerful reminder of how lucky I was to have grown up where I did. In this land where firmly held beliefs can sometimes violently clash, I found that people who value and love animals also hold a universal mutual respect for each other. This common value, the respect and love of animals, transcends language barriers, cultural differences, religious beliefs, and especially conflicting political opinions.

In my work with the Israeli veterinary community, it didn't make a difference if the animal owner was an Arab or a Jew. Everyone was treated with respect, and all the animals received equal care. I learned that when people keep the importance and love of animals in primary focus, they can overcome many of their differences.

Ask Dr. Mark:

Why Are Antibiotics Often Ineffective Against Bacterial Infections?

"I'll bet you a beer he'll be acting normal in twenty-four hours," the doctor jokingly dared me. I looked at the patient and didn't see how.

Dr. Rippin was the brother of the veterinarian who made it possible for me to be in Israel during the summer of 1978, between my third and fourth years of veterinary medical school. I was working with him for a week at a hospital in the city of Eilat, a beautiful resort destination on the shores of the northern tip of the Red Sea. (While this was my one unique experience during my time in Israel, I have had multiple opportunities to work alongside human physicians while I was working both my clinical years and with captive wildlife.) Here, the southernmost sliver of Israel borders Egypt to the west and Jordan to the east.

Being so close to the Sinai Peninsula, some of the patients at the hospital were Bedouin Arabs, people who lived mostly outside the realm of the modern world except to come to the city to seek medical care. The disease and surgical issues I encountered were those typically overcome by good preventive care in more developed communities. I felt as though I had stepped back in time.

The Bedouin patient in question had earlier been admitted to the emergency ward with a fever over 103°F. He was unresponsive and had neurologic signs compatible with severe bacterial meningitis, a condition where the covering around the spinal cord and brain is severely inflamed. In this case, the blood brain barrier that exists to safeguard the vital spinal cord and brain, being inflamed, loses its ability to be the protective barrier.

After the patient was evaluated and his initial blood work was back, Dr. Rippin asked me my opinion on the prognosis. Because I knew that a person or animal with symptoms as significant as the Bedouin's wouldn't have a good chance even to survive, I responded, "Very poor."

I took the bet to buy Dr. Rippin a beer mainly because I'd be elated if the Bedouin man was himself the next day. We administered a massive dose of penicillin and wrote orders for supportive care for the man through the night.

The next day on rounds, our patient was sitting up in his bed, eating and talking with a family member. I was astounded.

For years I'd heard lectures and read articles in medical publications on the negative impact of the overuse of antibiotics in both veterinary and human medicine. In 1978, my experience in the United States was that most bacterial meningitis infections were nonresponsive to penicillin. This was a result of its widespread use in both people and agricultural animals, or as many in the medical profession would say "overuse," which led to antibiotic resistance.

Antibiotic resistance is the ability of infectious organisms to adapt over time, making the drugs that were meant to kill or weaken them less effective. This can happen in repeatedly exposing microbes to the same antibiotic or when the drugs are inappropriately used.

In the case of the Bedouin patient, because his microbial system had experienced no previous exposure to penicillin, I got to see the miracle of a bygone era in the "advanced" modern world.

I happily bought Dr. Rippin a beer.

Chapter 5

GEORGE

"This dog has a diaphragmatic hernia," Paulette announced as she went about setting up an oxygen cage. Paulette had been a veterinary technician at Angell Memorial Animal Hospital for a decade, compared to my ten months as an animal doctor, so I found her presumptive diagnosis credible.

Angell Memorial, one of the nation's oldest animal hospitals, has been at the forefront of world-class veterinary care for over a century. The medical center was named to honor George Thorndike Angell, a lawyer active in the abolitionist movement who, after two horses were ridden so hard over forty miles they were quite literally raced to death, founded the Massachusetts Society for the Prevention of Cruelty to Animals in 1868, and helped to pass the state's first anti-cruelty laws.

The beautiful two-year-old German shepherd came into Angell just after midnight in the middle of a freezing Boston winter. Named George—like the hospital's namesake, George Angell—I felt a special affinity and responsibility to care for him. George arrived in the emergency room carried by his owner, Harold, a single, middle-aged man whose dog was not only his companion but also his best friend.

When I first saw George, it was evident he was in respiratory distress as he was having a hard time catching his breath. I immediately checked for a sucking chest wound that can be fatal very fast. It occurs when there is an open wound in the chest allowing air to be sucked into the chest with every breath, not allowing the lungs to expand. When I found no wound, I then checked his heart and airway passages looking for other traumatic reasons to explain George's difficulty in breathing. Once I confirmed that George was not in any immediate risk, I asked Harold what had happened.

"It's terrible. We were out for a quick walk, and George was playing around, barreling through a snowdrift that was six feet high." Harold was visibly shaken, but continued, "All of a sudden, a big snowplow turned the corner to plow the drift, and it hit George. It just threw him right in the air."

Angell Memorial handled over 50,000 cases a year and never closed its doors. Some emergency room incidents were so common they'd been given a term or even an acronym for short, such as HBC for "hit by car." In snowy New England, snowplow accidents had earned their own term, HBS for "hit by snowplow."

I asked Harold about any preexisting conditions. There were none, so I presented what the next steps would be so we could stabilize George and diagnose the extent of his injuries.

"Please, doctor, do whatever you can do to help George."

With Harold's go ahead, I ordered the radiographs. Most people call radiographs X-rays, but veterinary school ingrained in me that you don't see X-rays and you don't take X-rays. You take radiographs, and that's why the department is called Radiology.

At 1:00 AM, Paulette came over to help me position George for his radiographs. When the films were developed, they confirmed Paulette's diagnosis, showing the characteristic air bubble in the top part of the chest extending into the abdomen. The pressure created from being hit by a vehicle as large as a snowplow was so concussive to George's chest that it had ripped his diaphragm.

The diaphragm is a muscle that separates the chest from the abdomen in all mammals. When the abdomen contracts, it pulls the diaphragm down, creating negative pressure in the chest and expanding the lungs so they fill with air. The damage to George's diaphragm explained why he was having so much trouble breathing.

Miraculously, besides the life-threatening tear and a few broken ribs, George sustained only superficial bruises. The same snow that had hidden George from the view of the snowplow had, in fact, cushioned the blow and minimized any additional injury when he hit the ground.

To restore George's ability to breathe would require immediate surgery to repair the diaphragm. I went back into the room where Harold was waiting and explained the seriousness of the situation and why George was in an oxygen tank. He understood and consented to have me do the surgery. I was glad he didn't ask me how many diaphragms I had repaired.

As my intern rotation had me on a thirty-six-hour shift each week, I had successfully done my share of surgeries in the first six months of my internship. I had spent many nights on call, up all night accepting and caring for animals that walked, crawled, flew, swam, or in many cases were carried into the hospital. Being a veterinarian, a doctor that deals with a patient from birth to earth, means acting as a pediatrician to gerontologist; one minute I'd be dealing with a dog in heart failure and the next called to stabilize a hit-by-car (HBC) cat. However, I had never fixed a diaphragmatic hernia by myself. In fact, I had observed only one during my training at Cornell, when I watched another veterinary surgeon repair a torn diaphragm.

I could feel my self-doubt bubbling just below the surface, but Harold's confidence in me helped to quell my jitters. I also knew that the support staff were seasoned veterinary technicians who had my back, or more properly stated, had George's back. I turned my attention to stabilizing George and having him prepped for surgery.

Before I went to scrub in, I stole a few minutes to review notes on diaphragmatic hernia repair while the team prepared for surgery. Such surgery can be quite complex since the abdominal organs may have protruded into the chest cavity. If so, they need to be put back into position, and any tears in the diaphragm must be sutured closed.

By the time I was scrubbed in, with my stomach in my throat and somewhat nervous, I still felt as prepared as I could, and George was waiting for me on the table, anesthetized and prepped for surgery. I took a thorough accounting of everything around me and visualized the surgery I was about to perform. I followed that with an essential step: I took some very long cleansing breaths.

I then focused and picked up the scalpel and made the first incision along the midline of the abdomen, which is the approach to repair a torn diaphragm. Once I had access to the abdomen, I began pushing the stomach, spleen, and lobes of the liver aside so I could see the diaphragm. It looked like one of those small cereal boxes that open along perforated dotted lines, but in this case, the dotted lines were torn apart, and I was looking at lung tissue from the abdomen. The diaphragm was in three pieces.

I checked for any other damage to the lungs or throughout the abdomen. Finding none, I went to work sewing. In the medical field we call it suturing, but with a tear this dramatic, to me it felt more like sewing. I didn't count how many stitches I used to repair the tattered diaphragm, but I knew there were a lot because the surgery took almost two hours.

Finally, around 3:30 AM, George was back in the oxygen cage breathing easily. I found Harold anxiously standing by in the client waiting area. When he saw me enter the room, Harold stood up to receive the news.

"Harold," I said shaking his hand while putting my other hand on his shoulder to comfort him, "I'm delighted to let you know the surgery went well, and George is resting comfortably."

"Is he going to be all right?" Harold inquired nervously. "Yes," I assured him, "George is going to be fine."

As happy as Harold was, I cannot explain the jubilation I felt in having confronted a life-threatening situation and overcoming my self-doubt to surmount it. Although I was the surgeon at the helm, I knew it was only with the support of my experienced team members that the surgery was successful. Any veteran doctor knows to listen to trained technical staff during times of crisis. In the end, I think I have learned as much from support personnel as I have from professors.

George recovered in the hospital for three days. When he was well enough, I released him into Harold's care to go home with explicit orders to have minimal exercise for two weeks, not to be overexerted, and return for a recheck and suture removal in fourteen days.

Eight days later, I received an unexpected call from Harold. "Dr. Mark, you gave instructions that George's activity should be limited after his surgery, so I wanted to check with you on something I'm thinking about."

"Okay Harold, how can I help you?"

"I've wanted to breed George with a particular female German shepherd. She's just come into heat, so I was wondering if you'd consider that too much exertion for George."

I was so taken aback by the question that I asked one in return before answering. "Harold, do you breathe heavily when you take part in that type of behavior?"

No more words were necessary, and George went on to a full recovery.

To be a good doctor means staying constantly vigilant and looking for new opportunities to learn while having a healthy confidence in your ability to diagnose and treat. Successfully fixing George's diaphragmatic hernia was not only a learning experience for me in terms of technique, but also a rung on the ladder of building my self-confidence for helping the animals I cared so much about. I trusted in my teachers and believed in my abilities, and that made all the difference for George.

On the other hand, Harold's last question reminded me that no matter how clear your discharge instructions are, they can be misconstrued. As a veterinarian, you can't forget that your patients are animals, but it's the humans that you need to educate.

Chapter 6

FRANK

"I know there's probably nothing you can do," said the noticeably distraught middle-aged woman, "but I had to be sure."

Mrs. Lindsay had come to Angell Memorial Animal Hospital in the middle of a drizzly Boston day. She was my first appointment of the afternoon, and when she arrived one of the attendants went out to the car to help her bring in the patient. As Mrs. Lindsay and the attendant wheeled the patient in on a cart under a water-repellant drape, the juxtaposition of the situation struck me—not so much because it was raining, but because the patient's usual mode of transportation was swimming. It was ironic that a fancy goldfish needed to be shielded from rain when it lived in water.

Once everyone was in the exam room, I lifted the cover off the twenty-five-gallon aquarium and saw a striking orange and white fancy goldfish with a beautiful flowing tail.

The goldfish is a fancy, ornamental fish that is much more than the common goldfish you might win as a prize at the local fair and then unceremoniously and disrespectfully dispose of with a flush down the toilet. Fancy goldfish, in this case a fantail goldfish, were bred in China over a thousand years ago from wild carp originally cultivated for food. Over time, genetic mutations would occasionally produce a fish that was a brilliant red, yellow, or orange, and people began breeding them for such selective characteristics. As a result, today fancy goldfish can be found in a wide variety of body shapes and colors, with some measuring over a foot long and living up to twenty years. It's no wonder so many people around the world are captivated by these fascinating animals.

"I'm so sorry, doctor," said Mrs. Lindsay apologetically. "I know I must be wasting your time." She appeared to have been crying and was visibly distraught. Working in this field, I'd comforted many distressed clients, but Mrs. Lindsay seemed more shaken than most.

I looked at the goldfish and could see a multi-lobulated, pedunculate mass about one-quarter the size of the fish, located on its side contiguous with its gills. In other words, the fish appeared to have a large growth protruding from its body.

"Mrs. Lindsay, what can you tell me about your goldfish?"

"First of all, the goldfish is my son's pet. We got him about five years ago, and my son named him Frank."

"It appears Frank has a large growth on his side," I offered, "so I assume this must be the reason you're bringing him in."

"Yes, I know there's probably nothing you can do, but I had to at least try. You see, my son is severely autistic. His entire world revolves around this fish."

Mrs. Lindsay went on to explain that when her son got emotional and was unable to deal with a situation, he'd go and sit next to Frank, simply watching him, sometimes for hours. The mere act of doing so provided him great comfort, and he was able to settle down.

"Frank is one of the constants in his life that provides instant positive reinforcement. When he goes to feed the fish and Frank comes to the top of the tank, in his mind the fish is reacting personally to him. In my son's world, Frank never judges him and always, without fail, welcomes him when he comes over to the aquarium to watch him."

"My son learned to count by watching how many times Frank circled the tank," she continued. "He learned how important it was to eat because he understood it was important to feed Frank. He learned the importance of being clean because together we meticulously clean the glass and change the water, making sure it's the right temperature."

Mrs. Lindsay paused for a moment and took a breath. "Dr. Mark, when I explained to my son that Frank was going to the doctor because of the growth, his first response was 'what did I do wrong to make that happen?' So you see how important this is to our family."

Her comments made me have an epiphany. I realized that I was not only going to be responsible for the well-being of Frank, the goldfish, but also for the well-being of her son. I saw it as if I had two patients.

Then she said with tears in her eyes, "I can't replace Frank with another fish. My son would know the difference."

She kept repeating this, and so I wondered how many times she had been chastised after explaining to well-meaning friends and family why it wasn't silly to take a goldfish to the vet. I imagined she had heard the unsympathetic words, "You gotta be kidding me. That's crazy!" from those judging her actions.

I was sure she felt I might even be critical of her for bringing in an animal that could easily be replaced. Standing in the room, listening to Mrs. Lindsay and fully understanding how much Frank's well-being meant to her and her son, I realized then that she believed it was hopeless, and she felt helpless. At that moment,

I committed myself to doing whatever was reasonable and possible to rectify the situation.

I left the room and went back to the surgery department, where I found not one, but two surgeons free. Once they understood the nature of the medical case, both doctors wanted to come and see the fish. Like me, each of them approached the case with the same enthusiasm and professionalism they would with any other animal in need.

"Mrs. Lindsay, I'd like to introduce you to Dr. Mike Aronson and Dr. Joel Wolfson. We're going to work as a team to research and study the issue thoroughly and develop a course of action."

When Mrs. Lindsay heard this news, tears of joy replaced her tears of trepidation. Instead of ridicule and laughter, she realized we would take this case seriously and help as much as we could. I sent Mrs. Lindsay and the goldfish home with the promise of getting back to her with a plan of action in the next few days.

As a team, the other doctors and I poured through all the available medical literature, and I gathered information from an ichthyologist, or fish specialist, who was the curator at the New England Aquarium in Boston. From the team's research, the mass, given its location and appearance, would most likely be either a benign or malignant tumor, respectively a benign fibroma or a sarcoma, which would be malignant or cancerous.

There were challenges to the surgery, including how to safely anesthetize the fish and maintain it in a surgical plane of anesthesia, as well as how to control any bleeding during and after the excision. But we worked our way through the issues and within a few days developed a plan to surgically remove the mass.

I called Mrs. Lindsay to let her know the plan. Further, I was pleased to also be able to inform her that the Chief of Staff, Dr. Gus Thornton, had given me permission to cap the bill at $100.

We really had no experience, no idea, of what the outcome would be and arrived at this figure believing it was the fairest thing to do. What one couldn't put a price on was the intrinsic value of the fish to this family. Considering the fact it would take three doctors to do the surgery and a pathologist to identify the mass once removed, the $100 would be a small percentage of the actual cost.

"Thank you, Dr. Mark. I don't know what to say."

For everyone on the treatment team, not one of us ever second-guessed that we should do this. We weren't only treating a fish but a family in need.

The morning of the surgery soon arrived. Our game plan was straightforward. As the most experienced surgeon, Dr. Aronson would do the surgery with Dr. Wallach assisting, while I would be the anesthesiologist of record.

"All right, I'm going to start inducing anesthesia," I indicated to the team. "Frank is now going into a dilute concentration of Bromo-Seltzer." For the anesthetic, we had considered using an experimental drug, MS-222, or tricaine mesylate, which today is standard as an anesthetic for fish. At the time, however, it was still in the developmental stage, so we were concerned about its possible efficacy and toxicity. Instead, we had found evidence that Bromo-Seltzer, an antacid first produced in the late 1800s, had been successfully used to anesthetize fish for procedures lasting less than thirty minutes. We expected this operation to take far less than that amount of time, so we had chosen this as our anesthetic of choice.

"He's becoming sluggish," I reported in seeing Frank's movements slow down.

As the veterinarian assisting the procedure, Dr. Wallach's role was to hold the fish, a task not easily done. "Okay, I've got him," said Dr. Wallach as he gently picked up Frank and secured him in his gloved hands. The gloves were not only used for sterility but also served as a barrier against oils or any other substances on the holder's hands that could hurt Frank's scales or absorb through his gills.

With Frank safely in place, Dr. Aronson went to work. As he did, I continued to flush Frank's gills with a diluted solution of Bromo-Seltzer and water, which kept the fish anesthetized but allowed the gills to extract oxygen from the water so he could breathe.

"I've found the base of the pedicle where the mass is adhering to the gills," reported Dr. Aronson upon viewing the mass, which appeared like a mushroom with the stem being the pedicle. "I'm going to remove it now. Dr. Wallach, stand by to compress the surgical site."

We knew we needed to make the surgery as bloodless as possible since the fish did not have a lot to lose. We couldn't use anticoagulant chemicals to control the bleeding because they could hurt the fish if absorbed by the gills. Also, electric cauterization was naturally out of the question because of the wet environment. So the safest way to control bleeding was by direct compression, meaning to squeeze the fish, but not too hard, to avoid hurting him. Dr. Aronson excised the mass. Dr. Wallach next applied the appropriate amount of compression, and in no more than five minutes the removal was complete.

I quickly switched the fluid I was flushing over Frank's gills from Bromo-Seltzer to pure water. Dr. Wallach gently held Frank as we watched for signs of movement. In a few moments, the beautiful fancy goldfish started to squirm. Within minutes, we felt Frank was awake enough to swim under his own power and move water over his gills to breathe, so Dr. Wallach placed him into a tank of water we had standing by. Happily, Frank moved a bit slowly, but freely on his own.

The surgery was a success, with the mass removed and submitted for histological examination. We observed Frank for the remainder of the day, and by the evening we were comfortable he was doing fine. That night, we discharged him to go home with Mrs. Lindsay, along with instructions that if she or her son saw any unusual behaviors or secretions from the surgery site to call the hospital. Although we never got to meet Mrs. Lindsay's son, everyone on the staff who played a role in helping Frank knew they had done something special for a fish and this young man.

The next day I called Mrs. Lindsay to see how things were going "Oh, Dr. Mark, it's like a miracle!" She was ecstatic, reporting that Frank was acting normal and that her son felt his friend was more active than before the surgery. I wasn't surprised to hear this as I expected the mass had been weighing Frank down and affecting the gills. Because he was breathing better, he understandably had more energy, and I was glad to hear it.

We received more good news a few days later when the biopsy report came back with the finding that the tumor was a benign fibroma, not cancerous. Considering Frank's youthful age, hopefully he and Mrs. Lindsay's son would have many more happy years together.

I did a follow-up call six months later and found that Frank was doing fine. Like so many times in my career, it was a great day to be a veterinarian, knowing our team's work had purpose.

I first wanted to be a veterinarian to help animals. It was experiences like this that taught me that I was part of a sacred profession that had the ability to have a positive, meaningful impact on both animals and people.

Chapter 7

MEXICAN BOY

Most people don't realize that veterinarians are trained similarly to human physicians regarding medical conditions. Perhaps not being aware of this is why many people devalue the cost of providing veterinary care, which leads to many challenges veterinarians face on a daily basis. One time, the value of my training came to light in a profound way in an unlikely place.

My wife Kris and I were on vacation lounging by the pool on a picture-perfect day. The ocean water lapping on the nearby shore was that vivid blue color you only see in the Caribbean. The sky was nearly cloudless, and the sun warm but not overly. A week in Mexico was a romantic escape from our hectic lives, Kris working as a physical therapist and me as a veterinarian. Although we both loved our work, we were thoroughly enjoying a rare, relaxing moment to ourselves, fully engrossed in our books, without a care in the world.

"Ayuadame! Ayuadame!" A woman's cry broke the respite of an otherwise tranquil Cancún afternoon. Although I didn't speak Spanish, I knew this was a call for help. As I looked up, I saw the woman carrying the limp body of a young boy out of the swimming pool.

My years of emergency room training immediately kicked in, and I was instinctively jolted into action. As I got up to go to his side, I yelled for Kris to run and find help. My experience had taught me that the first thing to do in a crisis is to get more help. While Kris did that, I turned my attention to the young boy. I quickly ran to the crying woman and snatched the child out of her hands. At the same time, I tried to communicate to her with my eyes that the boy would be okay, even though I saw that he was blue and not breathing.

I went to work and first laid the youngster down on his back on the nearest beach chair. As I did so, I looked up toward the azure blue sky and said out loud, "Okay up there, I am going to do my job, and you will do yours. This boy is *not* going to die."

Everything I did next was as if I was on autopilot. I checked the boy's mouth for any obstructions. There were none. I felt for a pulse and discerned a very weak one.

Breathing air into his mouth twice, I got back great resistance. I then turned the boy on his side, and with a moderate amount of force I hit him twice on the back with an open hand on the area over his lungs.

Next, like clockwork, the boy gagged, and I held my breath. A moment later, he expelled what seemed to be an enormous amount of water for such a small boy. But those sounds of life and the water coming out of his mouth were the most glorious sight. He then gasped and started to breathe. As he did, I caught my breath as well. Although only a few minutes had passed in time, their intensity held me captive to only one thing: the young boy's well-being. As the child's color turned from pale blue to pink, I knew that *we* had won!

It was only then that I looked up and realized there was a sea of people all watching the drama unfold. I had been so focused on helping the boy that I was completely unaware of their presence. As I took in the gaze of bystanders looking on, a man holding a stethoscope rushed up and introduced himself as the hotel doctor. Kris had done her job. For a time in her youth Kris, had lived in Argentina and was bilingual, so she spoke to the doctor in Spanish as I picked up the boy and handed him to his mother.

The woman joyously wrapped her arms around the little boy as if she would never let go. We spoke different languages and couldn't communicate verbally. Instead, she looked at me, speaking with her eyes. So full of fear and despair just a few minutes earlier, they now communicated a tearful "thank you." I was still in a professional mindset, so I turned to the doctor and, with Kris's help, explained what had occurred.

With all of this behind me, I was suddenly overcome with a wave of emotions, almost to the point of not being able to stand. I turned to Kris and said, "I have to get away from the crowd." She took my hand, and we made our way to the other side of the pool, through the group of people that were starting to disperse. I sat down and looked out at the ocean and spontaneously began to shake and weep like a baby.

I did not feel like a hero. All I had done was what great teachers and experience had taught me to do. More than that, I was unexpectedly overcome with a feeling of spirituality unlike any I had ever known. Although raised in a Jewish home, I felt my upbringing had given me more a set of ethics and identity than becoming a deeply religious or "god-fearing" person. Yet at that moment I was overcome with gratitude. For one, I was thankful that I had simply been there and could help because of my medical training. I looked up at the sky again, remembering my directive plea from moments before, and said, "THANKS!"

The next day, Kris and I inquired about the boy with the hotel managers. They let us know the family had checked out and gone on their way. I never learned the boy's name, but he was okay, and we were at peace.

I was thankful for the knowledge and training others had passed down to me and the ability to rely upon it while trusting in a power greater than myself. Ironically, it was another moment in time that I was proud to be a veterinarian.

Chapter 8

CHARLES AND CAROL

"**Dr. Mark**," the receptionist indicated, "**your** next appointment is here. It's Mr. Kleinfeld."

"Thank you," I said and proceeded out to the clinic's waiting room at Angell Memorial Animal Hospital.

I found Mr. Kleinfeld seated on a chair with a shoebox in his lap.

"Hello Charles," I greeted him with a smile, "please come on back to the exam room."

Over the past few weeks, I had seen Charles and his cat multiple times.

On their first visit, when Charles had brought his feline friend in a shoebox into the exam room, the man looked very disheveled. None of his clothes matched or came close to fitting, and although he was clean, his overall appearance just seemed messy. It crossed my mind that he might even be homeless.

But I hadn't been there to judge Charles; I was there to help Carol, his cat.

When Charles lifted the lid on the shoebox, I saw Carol lying lethargically on her side. She was very thin with her ribs readily visible and her abdomen quite concave, like a bowl. On top of this, Carol seemed unwilling or unable to lift her head or respond to any stimulus, all of which were clear indicators this kitty was very ill, maybe even near death.

I had been trained to practice medicine by treating everyone equally, both my patients and their respective owners, so I proceeded to do a complete examination.

"Charles, what can you tell me about Carol?"

"Well, I noticed she was losing weight a while ago, but she seemed her usual self, so I figured she was fine. However, a few days ago she became very withdrawn and didn't have any energy, so I thought I'd better bring her in."

"I'm glad you did," I responded as I continued to examine the weak kitty. "Is Carol your only pet?"

"No, she's certainly not. I have twelve other cats, so there are thirteen in total at the house."

Okay, I thought to myself, *so I guess he's not homeless.*

I admit my mind immediately began to speculate about the living conditions at his house. I even wondered if he was a hoarder. All negative concerns were solely predicated on his appearance.

I went on to complete my examination.

The most significant and relevant finding was that Carol's kidneys appeared extremely small and irregular upon physical examination. Further, she was also mildly dehydrated, she had a rapid heart rate, and her breath had a very fishy odor characteristic of patients with uremia, a precursor to kidney failure.

"Charles, from my examination, I believe Carol's kidneys aren't working properly, and her condition is quite serious. Also, there's a palpable mass in her neck most likely compatible with a thyroid nodule. There may be other issues, but to understand this better will require a battery of tests."

I explained my recommendation to admit Carol to the hospital to fully diagnose and treat her. The tests I wanted to run would be used to not only assess the kidney problem and possible thyroid mass but also discover any other existing problems

I believe the art of practicing veterinary medicine includes providing every humane option when detailing the path an owner can take for dealing with a sick or injured animal. My approach was to offer *all* humane options regardless of variables like the financial and emotional resources of the client.

In this case, I provided a less costly option to run a more limited number of tests of just the kidneys to evaluate the most critical issues. Doing so would mean we'd be working under the premise there were no other problems, or at least leaving any less pressing issues undiagnosed for the time being.

In my practice, I never wanted to make assumptions about a client's motives for their decision-making. I considered it my job to present the options and support the pet family in the best possible way as long as the decisions were humane.

"Charles, as we've just discussed, I see two options for admitting Carol to the hospital; one, to run comprehensive tests to more thoroughly explore her health issues, or second, to run a more limited set of tests focused on just the kidney issues. In either of these scenarios, we would also treat her with IV fluids to address her dehydration."

I gently continued, "As difficult as it is for me to share this with you, I also want to add that in my opinion doing nothing isn't a humane alternative. Given Carol's critical condition, I believe this would only cause her to suffer greatly. So if for any reason the first two options of admitting her to the hospital for testing aren't doable, I would suggest you make the hard but loving decision to end her suffering now before it only worsens."

My guiding principle in such situations is that in return for the unconditional love we receive from our companion animals, or the beauty and purpose that all wildlife brings into this world, an animal entrusted to our care should never suffer unnecessarily. Further, I never left solutions out because I thought people might be offended, or couldn't afford them, or might not believe in them. I always strove to put all appropriate options on the table to be considered.

So in this instance, where Carol was suffering, and without medical intervention her condition would only continue to degrade, my view was that substantial treatment or euthanasia were the only viable options.

I explained this to Charles with the hope it might relieve any unnecessary guilt he might have felt about these options because, right or wrong, I expected him to choose the third option, euthanasia.

Although I like to think I don't let my biases affect how I practice medicine, like everyone, I still have them. And in this case, based primarily on Charles's appearance, I felt he might be too financially challenged to choose to admit Carol to the hospital for tests.

"Dr. Mark, if we stabilize the problems causing the uremia, what do you think the likelihood will be for successfully treating the mass in her neck? How many days in the hospital do you think it would take to see improvement?"

As Charles proceeded to ask insightful questions, I was impressed that he not only exhibited excellent understanding medically, but he did so with compassion.

"I believe there's a good chance Carol will respond to treatment, but of course, there are no guarantees," I said. "If we proceed, the tests and initial treatments will carry a substantial cost.

However, I believe we should be able to see how Carol's responding in a few days' time and can make adjustments accordingly."

Charles said, "I appreciate your approach to monitor her progress and make decisions as we go. That's how often I do things with my clients."

Clients? I thought to myself, caught off guard at the thought of Charles having clients.

"What kind of clients do you have?" I responded.

"Money brokers and others," he said and explained his role with his clients.

Here I was convinced that Charles was financially challenged, when, in fact, he was a very successful attorney, representing a variety of clients in all facets of the financial world, and was himself quite wealthy.

"Dr. Mark, I'm asking all of these questions because as much as I love Carol, I only want to proceed if it's fair to her."

"I understand, Charles. I would do the same thing in your shoes."

He responded, "I don't want to prolong or contribute to any suffering, but if there's a chance we can help her, I want to do it."

With Charles's go-ahead, we moved forward to work up a plan and admit Carol to the hospital.

She stayed for several days until all the tests had been conducted and the problems her kidney disease had created had been stabilized. I suspected Carol's dehydration was because she was losing more fluid than what she could ingest due to kidney failure, so we rehydrated her with intravenous fluids. The results of the tests found that Carol did indeed have kidney disease, but additionally, the blood work revealed she also had hyperthyroidism— an overactive thyroid, a disease that can advance in a cat to cause life-threatening heart problems.

To treat the hyperthyroidism, Carol would first need to be feeling stronger. Since she was doing well enough and didn't require further hospitalization, I sent her home for more recuperation time. I prescribed her some medications, a diet to help with her kidney disease, and also gave Charles instructions for continuing to give Carol fluids under her skin while at home. The administration would entail using a needle placed under the skin and attached by a hose to a sterile bag of fluid, to painlessly keep her hydrated as well as act as a simple form of dialysis.

Two weeks later, Carol returned to my exam room carried in the same shoebox by Charles.

"Dr. Mark, I want to thank you. Carol is doing much better."

As Charles removed the lid from the box, sure enough, Carol hopped out purring and began exploring around my exam room.

I could see Carol was ready for treatment of her hyperthyroid disease.

"Charles, because of the radioactive aspects of the treatment for Carol's hyperthyroidism, she'll need to spend five days in isolation."

I went on to explain the expenses, which would be high.

"Dr. Mark, I understand there will be some risks. Also, that the costs will be substantial, about $2,500 by the time we're done with the treatments, but that's okay."

"So you want to proceed?" I wanted to confirm.

"Yes, Dr. Mark." He then confided in me, "A few years ago I lost both my wife and my daughter to cancer. When that happened, everything changed for me."

The notion of a person losing their entire family in such a short time and at such a young age hit me like a ton of bricks. Suddenly, I saw Charles in a different light and felt as if I understood him in a new way.

His formula was a simple one. Losing his wife and daughter had profoundly changed what he wanted to do with the rest of his life and what he valued. He felt he didn't need much in material wealth. He didn't pay much mind to his appearance. He chose to live his life unorthodoxly from what the "norm" is.

"As strange as this may sound to some people, my cats are my family. They give me love and companionship, so in return, I'll do anything within my means to take care of them as best I can," he explained.

I could only imagine what phantoms of his past family may be haunting him with the current condition of his beloved cat, Carol.

"Charles, I believe in the power of the bond between people and animals. I've dedicated my life to this, and I seek to strengthen it in any way I can. I know Carol gives you unconditional love, and I admire your dedication to doing what feels right for you in taking care of her. I will be here to help all the members of your family as best I can." He looked me in the eye and shook his head in gratitude.

We moved forward in proceeding with the treatment, and Carol spent the next five days recovering in isolation. At the end of the five days, when Charles came for Carol at the hospital, he was so happy he acted like he was picking up a long-lost child he hadn't seen for ages. Carol purred at the sight of him, in a true bond of love and affection.

Over the course of the coming six years, I became familiar with Charles's entire family of cats. I came to learn that with every one of them, Charles had the same level of care and connection as he had with Carol and took care of them in the same way he had done for her.

During this time, it was on occasion also my role to assist some of Charles's cats over the Rainbow Bridge, the mythical bridge we like to envision we all cross to find our loved ones waiting for us in welcome on the other side.

Each time Charles had to say goodbye to one of his beloved cats, he was saying goodbye to a member of his family. I could only guess, but I sensed that somehow the pain of each loss he experienced was in some way balanced by the joy he received in other moments, especially when he'd introduce a new kitten to the family. To him, it was a recognition of the circle of life, with love and appreciation.

For the rest of my career, in my mind, thinking about Charles always reminded me to practice medicine the way I did with Charles and his cats; not to judge a book by its cover since clairvoyance was not taught in vet school, and to honor the power of the human-animal bond. It's this bond that can give someone strength in times of need, simply through the reciprocal acts of giving and receiving in love.

It was my honor to know this special man and his family. I hope the level of care I provided them equaled the invaluable insight Charles provided to me about what was truly important in life.

Ask Dr. Mark:

What Drives the Costs of Veterinary Care?

 Over the years, I've worked with countless people who must make very tough, sometimes life-and-death decisions, about the care of their animals, based in part on their financial resources. This lack of funds may require holding back a more expensive treatment or test, or taking a path that doesn't allow the animal to suffer unnecessarily. Because this is the reality many people face, I want to lend some understanding to a question I'm often asked: "Why does veterinary care cost so much?"

In the past three decades, the cost of providing good veterinary medicine have gone up precipitously. The reasons and issues regarding this would fill a number of textbooks, but I'll consolidate my explanation down to some basic facts.

Often forgotten, especially when a pet is sick or injured and the client is presented with the bill, is that the biological world doesn't care if the patient is an animal or human. Infectious diseases, injuries, cancer, or any other many maladies do not differentiate between humans or animals. Similarly, the skill to diagnose, treat, and hopefully cure, is the same no matter what the species. The skill of the medical staff, the cost of the materials and equipment, the sterility needed, and the general environment necessary for a favorable outcome for an animal are no different from what's needed in human medicine.

Additionally, it's not always evident to the client but a unique aspect of being a veterinarian versus other medical fields is that a vet in private practice must often own an *entire* hospital. There are few other medical professions where the general practitioner, or group of doctors, must own a hospital capable of handling client issues from infancy to old age. In other fields, when services are needed that require hospital services such as surgery, the patient is referred to a hospital facility not owned by the practitioner. But this isn't the case with veterinary medicine.

Even with the advancement of veterinary specialists, a general practitioner still needs an office that can support general medicine, as well as surgery, radiology, ultrasound, lasers, and basic ophthalmology and dental services, and emergency care. Each of these specialties requires a significant investment in both equipment and expertise. Also, the expertise is not only limited to the doctors but also to the technicians involved in the procedures.

Further, the initial investment in purchasing the equipment is only part of the story, as the ongoing upkeep and maintenance for it on an annual basis can also significantly add to the bottom line of running a full-service veterinary hospital.

Also to consider is the simple fact that the body of knowledge in veterinary medicine has grown exponentially, just as it has in human medicine—from pacemakers to prosthetics, kidney transplants to stem cells treatment. While this gives the practitioner a much greater ability to provide both preventive and interventional medicine, it also comes with more investments in equipment and training and often higher costs. The importance of this cannot be overemphasized, as even the most talented clinicians at the top veterinary hospitals in the world would miss things if they did not have diagnostic tests to understand what is truly happening with a patient that cannot talk and explain their symptoms or even hide them.

Such technological advances in veterinary medicine have had a very positive effect on outcomes. For instance, in the past vaccines for common diseases were given once a year, now they can be safely given every three years. Plus there's an enormous number of other medical and surgical problems that were unsolvable thirty years ago but that can now be cured or at least controlled.

This golden age of veterinary medicine has enabled our pets to live much longer and happier lives. That also means diseases that usually afflict the aged, such as cancer, are more common as our pets live longer. In turn, our pets are developing more complicated disease problems requiring new and more technologically advanced equipment. And more advanced technology means practitioners must acquire greater skill to diagnose and treat successfully, which all comes at a cost to the owner.

These are only some aspects of why the cost of veterinary medicine has increased in the last thirty years. Answers to this conundrum are on the horizon as medical insurance for pets, as is similarly available to humans, becomes more accessible, affordable, and applicable.

Chapter 9

OSCAR

"I'm so glad you're here, Dr. Mark," the nun said trembling. "Oscar's badly hurt. Can you see him?" Although I wasn't assigned to clinics that day at Angell Memorial Animal Hospital, I was able to free up the time, so I met them in my examining room.

Oscar was a lovable, long-haired ball of shaggy tan fur. His tail never stopped wagging, and anyone close by would be on the receiving end of an exuberant lick of his long tongue. He resembled a terrier breed, weighing in around forty-five pounds, and had been in my care as a patient since he came to my office for his initial vaccinations and neutering as a puppy. In the years since that first visit, I'd seen Oscar many times for annual examinations and heartworm tests. He was always the happy-go-lucky dog, and with good reason: he'd hit the lottery in having a wonderful home.

Oscar had been adopted by an order of Catholic nuns in Jamaica Plain, a suburb just southwest of downtown Boston. The sisters idolized him. Oscar not only provided them unconditional love, but he also entertained them with his nonstop antics. Every time Oscar came in for a visit I would hear stories of his capers, such as his stealing an article of clothing from one nun and hiding it in another sister's room, which provided them hours of hide-and-seek fun and great laughter all around.

As soon as I saw Oscar in the examination room, it was immediately clear he wasn't his usual jovial self. "Sister Elizabeth, can you tell me what happened?" I asked while checking the dog's vital signs. Over the years, I had developed a friendship with Sister Elizabeth. She was his primary caretaker who, along with the other nuns, gave Oscar lots of attention and excellent care.

"I feel so guilty," Sister Elizabeth started as she distraughtly explained how Oscar had somehow gotten out of their building.

The convent was close to Jamaica Pond, a beautiful freshwater body of water rimmed by parks very popular with Bostonians out for a walk and ducks for a swim. Oscar and the sisters were frequent visitors to this place, so he knew it well. He was especially enamored of the ducks and, apparently, their siren call was so powerful he simply couldn't wait for his next supervised outing. To get to the park, however, Oscar had to cross Jamaicaway, a heavily trafficked parkway. Unfortunately, his front end made it across the street, but his back end got clipped by a car. The nuns were aware immediately that he had escaped and saw the accident happen from across the street. They were devastated. As quickly as possible, the nuns rushed him to Angell Memorial, which, fortunately, was just minutes down the road.

Luckily, Oscar's vital signs were okay. After a thorough evaluation, including X-rays of his chest and abdomen, I was able to comfort the nuns that there were no immediate life-threatening issues.

The nuns were relieved, but Oscar still wasn't in good shape. His back right leg was severely mangled, and the lower limb felt like a bunch of unattached bones in a sock due to multiple fractures. Repairing the broken bones would require the services of an orthopedic surgeon to fix them with internal pins and wires. Sadly, that would be the easy part. Of greater concern, the leg had also sustained what's known as a "degloving" injury. The term relates to picturing how a glove comes off a hand, but in this case, it was the skin around Oscar's lower limb and paw that was stripped back off of the leg. Degloving injuries are all too common when a vehicle hits an animal. The injury often requires major surgical interventions, or in certain cases even amputation. For the animal, the recovery and healing period can be long and painful due to the significant trauma and damage to soft tissues and blood supply.

Today, reconstructive surgery on animals is commonplace, but it was new territory in the 1980s when this incident occurred. Fortuitously, during this same era at Angell Memorial, Dr. Michael Pavletic was pioneering such techniques. Dr. Pavletic had become interested in surgery during his internship—just a short time before my own interning—when he met a cat that had a tumor on its face. At the time, the available conventional methods made it impossible to close the wound after removing these types of tumors from an animal. However, Dr. Pavletic approached the challenge by thinking outside the box. For inspiration, he turned to a reconstructive surgery textbook from human medicine that suggested a simple skin flap might work. He then tailored that routine technique for humans into a procedure for a cat. Brilliant!

I knew Dr. Pavletic would have the expertise to best address getting Oscar's skin to grow back, so I talked through the options for treating the issues with the nuns. We discussed everything from simpler and less expensive approaches, to those including skin grafting and reconstructive surgery, the latter of which would come at a very significant cost. We explored all of the various options, but Sister Elizabeth would not consider anything less than whatever was the absolute best for Oscar. Without hesitation, she said, "You cannot put a price on love!" So we moved forward.

There were many things we had to do to prepare for the initial surgery. Because Oscar would be at risk for infection over the coming months of multiple surgeries and his healing and recovery, I started treatment by putting him on long-term antibiotics. In the first few days, Oscar's dressing had to be changed and debrided to remove any dead, damaged, or infected tissue from the area. Debridement not only cleans the wound of such unwanted material but also promotes the healing potential of any remaining healthy tissues. From there, Oscar's dressing changes were stepped down to every three days and so on as his leg improved.

Over the course of three months, Oscar was in and out of the hospital and was treated with tender, loving care as Dr. Pavletic performed multiple reconstructive skin-grafting surgeries with tremendous skill, and the nuns held prayerful vigils for their furry friend.

As Oscar continued to improve, Sister Elizabeth was effusive in her thanks and admiration for all the veterinarians and veterinary technicians who helped with her beloved pet's care. Ultimately, Angell Memorial also absorbed some of the costs in recognition of the convent. In return for the kindness of each contributing individual and the hospital at large, every week Sister Elizabeth brought fresh-baked cookies for the staff to enjoy.

To this day, I believe it was the combination of exceptional surgery skills and the care provided by everyone at Angell Memorial, combined with the outpouring of love and vigilant prayers from the nuns that allowed Oscar to return to normal.

Finally, it came time to declare Oscar healed. It was a happy moment to celebrate as he came in for his final visit. I removed all his bandages and then smiled with hugs all around as we sent

Oscar on his way home with tail wagging and tongue ready to express his gratitude with lots of wet, sloppy kisses.

I was surprised the next day when I received a call from Debbie, the front office person at Angell Memorial saying that Sister Elizabeth was there wanting to see me. "Dr. Mark, she doesn't want to take much of your time, but she's come to give you a gift, a very personal and meaningful gift."

I was in the library located on the other side of the campus from the hospital's main entrance, easily a quarter of a mile away. I told Debbie I was on my way, but it would take me some time to make the trek over. As I walked, knowing that the sister was there to give me a gift, I was feeling uncomfortable.

First of all, I felt Oscar's recovery was my reward. What motivates most of the veterinarians and veterinary staff with whom I've had the privilege to work is seeing the results of their efforts in helping an animal and their family, especially when it's to prevent or relieve an animal's suffering. Because of this, I've never been very comfortable accepting any additional gifts for my work.

I also felt awkward accepting a gift just for me, because I knew that Oscar's recovery was a result of a talented cast of many skilled and caring professionals. While I was the point person and primary clinician, the outcome was nevertheless very much a team effort, particularly considering Dr. Pavletic's pivotal role in helping Oscar. Dr. Pavletic similarly went on to help an untold number of animals as one of the "founding fathers" of veterinary medicine, one instrumental in pioneering dozens of reconstructive surgery techniques used around the world to this day. So, like other times I've been the recipient of generous gifts of appreciation, I felt undeserving of individual recognition.

As I continued walking to the main entrance, I had plenty of time to prepare myself to be grateful and gracious, but instead of focusing on that, my mind went off on a tangent. I started thinking about Sister Elizabeth being a nun, and how she might want to present me with a gift of symbolic meaning or religious significance. The idea took over my thoughts so much so that by the time I got to where she was waiting, I was sure I would soon be the recipient of Rosary beads, a Bible, or another religious book. Assuming this, and being a spiritually Jewish person, I began to prepare myself to accept something that—albeit given with the best of intentions—I might not identify with. All these thoughts floated through my mind, especially Debbie's resounding words, "A very personal and meaningful gift."

When I finally got to my destination and opened the lobby door, I was greeted by a joyful Oscar, jumping up and down, barking with unbridled excitement. Except for the hair growing back on his leg in a slightly incongruous fashion because of the multiple skin grafts, you would never have been able to tell from his behavior that he had been severely injured. He greeted me as if I were his best friend rather than the person who was primarily responsible for putting him through numerous painful bandage changes. Oscar was the perfect example of recognizing and acknowledging gratitude, something that many of our animal friends often do better than we humans.

"Dr. Mark, thanks for coming to meet me," Sister Elizabeth said as she handed me a gift-wrapped box. I smiled and thanked her as I accepted the box, which was quite heavy. I slowly lifted the lid, ready to show my appreciation no matter the gift. Foolishly enough, I was completely unprepared for the reality of its contents. Inside was a beautiful, smooth gray stone, meticulously hand painted by Sister Elizabeth. On it, in a rainbow of colors, was a collage of pretty flowers, a Jewish star, and in bold letters the word *SHALOM,* the Hebrew word for "peace," "hello," and "goodbye."

Looking back decades later—and at the stone still resting in my fountain—I still feel it's one of the most meaningful gifts I have ever received. Given the unfounded trepidations I had as I walked toward the front office that day, it is probably also one of the least deserved. In sharing their heartfelt gift, Sister Elizabeth and the other nuns at the convent had provided a truly powerful lesson about sincere love, abiding loyalty, and genuine thought-fulness. I shall treasure those gifts forever.

Chapter 10

FRANCIS

 **"He's named after Saint Francis of Assisi," Ms.** Franklin said as she introduced me to her beautiful, loving German shepherd. Her dog Francis was nine years old and named for the patron saint known for his love of animals. Ms. Franklin was a single, middle-aged Irish woman who was a religious Catholic and loved her dog like family. She had brought Francis into Angell Memorial for hot spots while I was working at the hospital as a senior clinician.

Hot spots, also known as acute moist dermatitis or canine pyoderma, are oozy, reddish sores or areas of inflammation of the skin. In this case, the location of the hot spots was at the base of Francis's tail, and the black particles on and around the hot spots were diagnostic of an infestation of fleas.

One of the many differences in practicing medicine for animals versus people is that a veterinarian's diagnosis and plan of treatment must be accepted not only by the patient themselves but also by the owners. This is important because it's the owners who must understand the problem and take responsibility for implementing any treatments once they've left the hospital.

When a dog has hot spots from a flea infestation, showing an owner the black particles, which closely resemble grains of black pepper, can be helpful to persuade the hesitant client to accept that their dog has fleas. By taking some of the dark particles and putting them on a white paper towel or tissue, they'll turn into red spots. That very distinct red color is dried blood, or in this case, the fecal excretions left behind by the fleas.

When I showed Ms. Franklin the red spots, she accepted the diagnosis, and we discussed the treatment. Therapy for Francis would include ministering a soothing antiseptic ointment on the affected areas and appropriate flea control, as well as a proper treatment of his environment to eradicate fleas in and around the home.

"Thank you," said Ms. Franklin as she started to collect her things to leave. "I'm very grateful to know the problem can be solved."

"Before you go, Ms. Franklin, I'd like to ask a few more questions." I paused and took a breath.

A skilled clinician is trained to look at the whole patient when presented with a problem, and from the moment they first lay eyes on them. In most cases, a clinician will leave working up the problem for last after taking in as much information as possible. So in this instance, it wasn't a case of hot spots that entered the room to be treated. It was Francis as a whole. At the time Francis initially walked in, I observed that his rear end acted like it was separate from his front end in the way it swayed back and forth. His gait was such that it was typical of a devastating disease that German shepherds have a higher incidence of than other breeds. While examining the dog for hot spots, I also conducted an entire physical exam that included some neurological tests.

"Ms. Franklin, I noticed the way Francis is walking, how his hips are swaying unusually. Have you noticed this, and, if so, how long has it been since you first detected it?"

"I saw the swaying in the past few months. I just assumed it was due to his age, she said." I asked a few more questions about his gait and how he walked. "Well, now that you mention it," Ms. Franklin continued, "I've observed that he has difficulty picking up his hind end after lying down."

My heart sank as I took in her answer and finished the exam. Given all the information, I knew that Francis most likely had a disease called German shepherd myelopathy, or GSM. This is a degenerative disease comparable in humans to amyotrophic lateral sclerosis, otherwise known as ALS or Lou Gehrig's disease. For dogs, GSM is a progressive, noninflammatory degeneration of the white matter of the spinal cord. It's most common in German shepherds and Welsh corgis but is occasionally recognized in other breeds. As the disease progresses, it eventually leads to paralysis in the hind end and incontinence, the same condition in humans that requires adult diapers. The progression can be highly variable, but the dog's history and findings of my examination of Francis led me to believe that, in his case, the degeneration was proceeding rapidly.

It's always hard for a veterinarian to discuss terminal diseases with a client, but it's especially hard to bring up when it's unexpected. "Ms. Franklin," I said with care, "I know you brought your dog in for hot spots, and I'm glad we have a plan for addressing that issue. However, after examining Francis and talking with you further, it's my opinion that it's very likely he also has a condition known as German shepherd myelopathy."

She shook her head and asked, "What's that?" After I explained the condition, she was naturally taken aback by this totally unexpected outcome. After the initial shock wore off, she said, "Okay Dr. Mark, if Francis has GSM, how do we treat it? What can be done for him?"

"Unfortunately Ms. Franklin, that's the worst of it. Despite all the medical advances, in the case of GSM there is no treatment for it. I'm very sorry." Understandably, the news shook her, and she began to cry.

I kept my own emotions in check and explained to Ms. Franklin that I'd like to take some X-rays of Francis's back and hips as well as do other general lab tests. She agreed to that, and also to my suggestion that we have the neurologist evaluate Francis to confirm the diagnosis. Unfortunately, as expected, the tests confirmed the diagnosis as progressive degenerative myelopathy in a German shepherd.

A veterinarian in practice often deals with life and death on a daily basis, sometimes even two or three times in a row. It may even become "routine" because that's the cycle of life, but it never becomes easy. It's simply one of the burdens that come with being an animal doctor.

Despite the shock of such bad news in cases like GSM, everyone must focus and keep moving forward. So Ms. Franklin and I developed a plan. We treated the hot spots, and since there were no treatments for GSM, Francis would simply go home. Moving forward, I would see Francis every three weeks to assess the progression of his disease.

Three weeks later I saw Francis right on schedule. In that short amount of time, the progression of the disease was evident in the lack of control that he had over his back legs. As the weeks went by, at every visit I could see the degeneration advancing in Francis and the toll it was taking on Ms. Franklin. Francis was her best friend.

His condition continued to get worse, with other side effects coming to the surface. Nine weeks after the first office visit, Francis was dragging his hind end and was also incontinent, which led to urine scalding on his rear quarter. Two weeks later, Francis had fly larvae, or maggots, in the sores on his hind end, and the area was very painful when it was touched. I admitted him to the hospital that day and cleaned out the maggots and treated the sores. Throughout the procedure, it was obvious the whimpering dog was in great pain.

Afterward, I found Ms. Franklin in the waiting room so we could have a discussion. This sort of talk would be like the many consultations I had held before with other families, but it's never easy. However, given Francis's condition, I felt it was time to discuss end-of-life issues. My approach in practicing medicine with animals is that in return for their unconditional love, endless work, or the fact they are sentient beings that feel pain, it is our moral obligation not to allow them to suffer needlessly. In some cases, where the condition is terminal and the animal is experiencing tremendous pain and discomfort, I believe the most appropriate and humane course of action is euthanasia. As Ms. Franklin and I talked about the situation and the option of ending Francis's life, and in spite of her deep caring and flowing tears, I came to realize that as a devout Roman Catholic she could not accept euthanasia as a solution to end Francis's pain. I respected her decision at the time and sent Francis home.

Five days later, Ms. Franklin called and asked if I would see Francis again because the maggots had returned causing terrible discomfort. I asked her to bring the dog to the hospital immediately. From the time Ms. Franklin called until she got there, I did some soul searching. I knew how Francis would look and feel when he arrived. His hind end would be dragging with multiple sores caused by urine scalding and infestation with maggots. With these thoughts in mind, I decided to do something I'd never done before. When Ms. Franklin arrived, I met her outside with a cart so that Francis wouldn't have to drag himself into the hospital. Then for the first and only time in my career, I asked Ms. Franklin to accompany me back to the treatment room and hold Francis while we cleaned him up.

It tore me apart inside to expose her to the harrowing scene of what Francis endured as we cleaned him. Despite this, I felt she needed to understand the truly horrific discomfort her cherished pet was going through in removing the maggots. While some might disagree with me for taking this approach, I felt it was necessary information for Ms. Franklin so she could make the most humane decision for Francis. She only had to experience this sight for a few minutes before asking me to step outside so we could talk.

Noticeably shaken and with tears streaming down her face, Ms. Franklin looked at me and said, "Please take him out of his misery." I looked at her and comprehended the emotional devastation she was experiencing, then confirmed that she understood we would be euthanizing Francis. She tearfully nodded yes. I hugged her to assure her that she was making the most selfless and best decision for her companion. It was her love for Francis that was giving her the strength to go forward with relieving his severe pain and misery. She then came into the treatment room and said her final goodbyes, crying bittersweet tears for the great loss of her best friend and the relief of his misery.

To this day, I don't question my decision to expose Ms. Franklin to the full measure of her pet's discomfort. I will always respect her beliefs and appreciate how her love for her best friend enabled her to unselfishly relieve his misery in spite of the moral dilemma it caused for her.

Ms. Franklin represents countless numbers of people I have seen during my career who deeply love their animals and have to make that very hard decision. I thank every one of them for the decision to remove interminable suffering when there is no other available solution of relief. In my heart, I believe the decision to end the life of a suffering individual is one of the greatest acts of kindness and love that I know.

In ancient Greece, the definition of euthanasia was "an easy or happy death." In modern times, this sentiment is echoed when doctors assist in relieving a patient's suffering from an incurable and painful disease.

Although St. Francis of Assisi was a symbol from a faith different than mine, when it came time to end the suffering of Ms. Franklin's best friend, I wanted to think that a patron saint of animals was watching over Francis the German shepherd that day and welcoming him home. This lesson reinforced for me why veterinarians play such a critical role in offering comfort to both people and animals even in the most difficult circumstances.

Chapter 11

HAROLD

"Doctor, are you familiar with hamsters?" the boy asked me one rainy, cold November morning. David was ten years old, and he and his mother, Janie, had brought his hamster into my exam room at Angell Memorial Animal Hospital.

"Yes, I am," I replied. "I've treated a number of them over the years." From the smile on his face, my response appeared to give him some comfort.

"This is Harold," David said as he took the cover off the shoebox. He reached in and gently picked up the animal, being very careful not to hold the back left leg. The box was lined with torn white paper towels to keep Harold comfortable, but I could see the sheets of paper stained with some dry blood.

David showed me the problem on the back leg and then gently placed his furry friend back in the shoebox. It was obvious that Harold didn't want to use that leg at all. The foot was swollen, and there was a large mass that appeared to be an ulcerated lesion involving the entire lower limb, which likely explained the blood on the paper towels.

"What can you tell me about Harold?" I asked.

"Well, Harold is a year old," David said. "He stays in my room so I can take care of him. Every day I feed him his hamster food pellets, but on the weekends I give him a treat, like a small piece of carrot or half a grape. He loves those." David went on to explain how much water Harold drank, what kind of wood chips were in the enclosure, and how often the hamster's cage was cleaned. He even knew how much waste material Harold produced and what it looked like. I was very impressed. Despite his age, David was the perfect client. He knew the needs of the animal he cared for and was a great historian.

While he was talking, I examined Harold just as I would any other animal. In doing so, I sensed that David and his mom appreciated that I took Harold's health seriously even though he was a small hamster, an animal that can be replaced for a couple bucks at a pet store and some would consider vermin. As a veterinarian, I took an oath that I would use my knowledge and skill to benefit society through the protection of animal health and welfare, and that I would prevent unnecessary suffering and relieve it whenever possible. Nowhere in the oath does it delineate that this applies to only certain species. To David and his mom, Harold was part of the family, a prime example of the human-animal bond.

I proceeded to do a complete physical exam except for taking Harold's temperature, as hamsters are susceptible to prolapsed rectums. Otherwise, I listened to his heart and lungs with a stethoscope, weighed him, and conducted an oral exam. I left examining the hurt leg for last. Unless it's an emergency, it's typically best to leave the obvious problem until the end of the exam so that one doesn't miss something else while being absorbed by the conspicuous issues. It also keeps any discomfort that might occur to a minimum when you examine the problem.

"David, what can you tell me about Harold's leg?" David

explained when he first noticed there was something wrong with the leg and gave a comprehensive history of how it progressed.

Like other veterinarians, I follow the S.O.A.P. format as one my most important clinical tools. S.O.A.P. stands for **S**ubjective observation, **O**bjective observation, **A**ssessment, and **P**lan. This approach is a universally accepted way of practicing medicine when presented with a patient with a problem.

In this case, my *subjective* findings were an obviously swollen left hind leg that appeared to be invasive to the entire lower limb. My *objective* findings were that the leg didn't look broken. Further, Harold was not exhibiting any systemic signs of disease, such as fever, and with David's excellent history, it seemed Harold still had his normal amount of energy. I also knew he was eating well and not losing weight.

Based on this, my *assessment* was that this was either a localized infection, a compromise of the circulatory system in the hind limb, or a tumor of unknown etiology. However, given all the facts, the most likely conclusion for me was that this was a mass of the lower limb and was acting as if it was a malignant tumor or cancer. Further, nothing from the history, exam, and my knowledge allowed me to suggest that the process in the leg would resolve itself spontaneously. I let David and Janie know my assessment. When they heard the news, they took a moment and held hands.

"Given the findings here with Harold's leg, I believe there are three humane options to consider taking at this time."

When developing a *plan,* in most complex medical cases there are often many options. To develop a course of action includes considering many things, not the least of which is the quality of life for the animal, along with weighing the chances of success and possible outcome with the owner's emotional and financial resources available for whatever strategy is presented and elected. In this case, I was sensitive to the fact that I was talking to a boy who was very knowledgeable and attached to his hamster. At the same time, I didn't want to forget his mother and her desires. Depending on the approach, there could be considerable differences in financial obligations, so I was conscientious to make sure I had her permission to present all the options. I wanted to be respectful, as well as not create expectations or unnecessary guilt by providing options that could not be considered at all.

"It's okay, Dr. Mark," Janie said. "Let's hear all the options." Perhaps she knew her son better than I could fathom or felt it was meaningful he make an informed decision. In any case, she plainly felt the boy was mature enough to hear all the considerations.

"The good news is that while Harold may have some discomfort now, I have no reason to think he's suffering," I said, then continued, "but it's difficult to know when that could change." The pair looked at me and nodded that they understood. "So one option would be for Harold just to go home and we'll see how things go. However, as his condition progresses it will be important for you to pay attention to any signs that may indicate he's beginning to suffer. You can tell by being aware of his vocalizations, whether he's losing weight or has a loss of appetite, or other significant changes in his behavior. Also, if he can't keep himself clean or shows signs of not caring, such as being withdrawn and depressed. Those would be indicators as well."

As the thought of what Harold was facing started to sink in, the sorrow of David and his mother openly crept into their faces. I explained that at such time it became evident Harold was suffering, there would be the option to relieve his pain by humanely ending his life. I further explained that without significant intervention, the disease affecting Harold's leg would proceed rapidly.

In accepting that reality, another option would be to end his life humanely now. Doing so would serve to relieve the family of any doubt as to whether they were allowing Harold to suffer without them knowing.

"Alternatively, we can look at doing surgery on his leg to remove the mass. However, although it's my clinical impression that we can attain a longer pain-free life for Harold, I'm not fully confident it'll cure the problem."

"Dr. Mark," asked David's mom, "how much would this cost?"

"It will be expensive. First we need to ensure surgery isn't con-traindicated by doing some X-rays and blood work. Then there's the cost of the operation, plus a biopsy and lab work."

"I see," she said.

When he heard all the information, David paused for a moment and then turned to his mother. "Mom," he said, "The money I've been saving from my newspaper route these past two years so I could get a bike, I think it's enough to pay for Harold's care. I want to do that. I can wait another year to get the bike."

It was all I could do to not show my emotion. I was a young boy once and knew what it was like to dream about getting a new bike. Suddenly, to me, David was no longer a boy but a young man.

I knew that this would not be routine for the surgeons and that Harold might not survive the operation, so I turned to Janie and asked her to join me in the hall. "We're only going to charge $25 for the surgery," I told her. "After all, it's microsurgery." In reality, microsurgery was much more expensive, plus the ancillary costs, but that didn't matter to me.

"Really?" she said with a surprised grin. "Are you sure?"

"Yes, but in return, I want you to promise that you'll get David a shiny new bicycle for Christmas."

"Absolutely," she happily agreed with a joyful tear.

We scheduled the surgery, and they returned in a short while for the procedure. It went off without a hitch, and Harold uneventfully returned home minus his painful left leg. In a few days, the tumor microscopic report came back as a fibrosarcoma, a form of cancer. I felt elated we had made a favorable choice in removing the leg.

Six months later I received a card in the mail from David. Drawn on the front was a picture of his three-legged hamster friend. Inside the card was a handwritten message that read, "Dear Dr. Goldstein: Harold died last night in his sleep, but I am so happy we helped him."

Hamsters typically only live for three years. Although sad to hear of Harold's passing, I was happy to have been able to help in extending his life and witness the loving acts of a wonderful boy.

I don't know what David is doing today, but it's my belief that he's grown up to be a caring and thoughtful person, providing a positive impact on the lives he touches. He chose a pain-free life for his hamster instead of a shiny new bike. At that moment, he influenced both the way I practiced medicine from that day forward and, in fact, how I have made decisions in my own life. It was a lifelong lesson in values from a ten-year-old boy.

Chapter 12

TOLERANCE

 "They never taught us how to deal with this in vet school!" Dr. Hall cried out in exasperation.

The young doctor was clearly upset, so I gave her a moment to calm herself before asking what the problem was.

"My client's yelling at me! She called me morally bankrupt and demonic," Dr. Hall huffed. "The woman accused me of saying her kittens are immoral!"

Dr. Hall was just starting her highly coveted internship at Angell Memorial Animal Hospital, excited about beginning her career at the equivalent of Harvard or the Mayo Clinic for human medicine. Her clinical proficiency gained in college made Dr. Hall a top candidate for acceptance into Angell's limited internship program, but her veterinary training hadn't necessarily prepared her to handle the misconceptions that clients can have about animals or to be the target of verbal bashing.

"I understand why you're upset," I said. "What are the client's concerns?"

I knew from personal experience that pet owners could sometimes have extreme beliefs or behaviors. For instance, I once had a woman come to see me because she was convinced that her cat was female, despite the expert opinions of two other veterinarians who each concluded the kitty was male.

"It started off as a routine exam. A woman brought in her new kittens for their first vaccinations and a check-up," said Dr. Hall.

The kittens were a brother and sister from the same litter, both eight weeks old. Dr. Hall conducted a full physical examination on each kitten and provided the client with information on vaccinations, nutrition, litter box issues, and general behavior.

"Are you planning to keep the cats indoors?" Dr. Hall asked the client.

"Yes, we'll be keeping them indoors."

"That's good. I strongly recommend for cats to be indoors as it is much safer for them. Also, they have each other to play with, and you can keep an eye on their health much more easily. However, even though the kittens won't be going outside, it's still important they be spayed or neutered at the appropriate age."

"I heard that neutering would help to prevent a boy cat from spraying in the house," the woman said.

"Yes, it can often remedy those issues, but there are many other reasons to spay and neuter, especially in this case where the two may breed with each other."

The woman looked confused for a moment.

"As I told you, doctor, we intend to keep the kittens indoors at all times," she said, then quickly escalated to a roar, "If you are suggesting they would have sex with each other, may I remind you, doctor, they are brother and sister!"

Although rattled by the client's aggression, Dr. Hall calmly replied, "I understand. However, although they are brother and sister, that will not inhibit them from breeding."

The woman turned red, looking as though she'd blown a gasket, and shouted, "Are you suggesting my beautiful innocent kittens would be *incestuous?* Because if you are, then you are insulting my kittens and me, by accusing them of being immoral, and I will never come back here again!"

The woman went on, but at that point Dr. Hall thought it best to exit the room to regain her composure and seek out advice, the kind they don't teach you in school.

I assumed Dr. Hall understood that her client was anthropomorphizing, or attributing human characteristics and purposes, to her kittens, but I offered a few thoughts on the subject anyway to give her the chance to talk about it.

"Thank you for the listening ear, Dr. Mark," Dr. Hall warmly said. "I became a vet because I love animals and want to help them. I never expected this kind of interaction with a client. I appreciate you reminding me that understanding and communicating well with people are a big part of the equation in my providing care for their animals."

Dr. Hall then returned to the exam room, politely and professionally concluding the appointment with the client.

Over the years this story became the example I would often share with individuals thinking of going into veterinary medicine.

Being a good veterinarian takes a lot more than loving animals. Pets don't take themselves to the vet or have a wallet or a purse with which to pay for their own care. It takes being a people person as well, being patient, understanding, and listening to all, even when the situation seems surreal or confrontational.

Chapter 13

SASHA

**One of the big draws at the Stone Zoo in** Boston was Sasha, a Siberian tiger. Zoo visitors fell in love with her as a cub. Sasha had started life weighing only two pounds. She had been one of two female Siberian tiger cubs born to their mother, Segezha (see-ge-zhuh), in May 1976 at the Stone Zoo in Boston. However, shortly after the birth, Segezha had rejected both her newborn daughters.

Tigers are the largest of all wild cats and Siberian, or Amur, tigers are the largest in the world. The largest Siberian tigers have been known to reach over ten feet in length nose to tail and, when fully grown, weigh in at 700 pounds. In the wilderness reaches of Russia's far eastern forests, where Siberian tigers freely roam in their natural habitat, being a rejected cub would've spelled certain death. Born temporarily blind, young tiger cubs are completely reliant on their mothers for food and protection, remaining in their mother's care and training for two to three years until they venture out on their own as young adults. But in a Boston zoo, Segehza's rejection meant that Sasha would be a tiger cub hand raised by human caretakers. As the months progressed under their watchful care, by the following January Sasha was a seventy-pound, eight-month-old that loved to romp in the New England snow with zoo staff.

Siberian tigers are rare, and beautiful cub Sasha had been an instant hit with visitors and keepers alike. Being accustomed to humans, she grew to not only be tolerant but affectionate toward them, often providing a series of pleasant purring sounds and curling her lips as if to smile. Both are friendly behaviors exhibited by tigers. Unfortunately, she did not display such behaviors toward the veterinarians who treated her because, sadly, in her first year of life Sasha had been diagnosed with chronic pancreatitis.

In mammals, the pancreas is an organ responsible for producing enzymes needed for digestion and also contains the pancreatic islet cells, which produce insulin. In a patient with pancreatitis, the same digestive enzymes depended on to help digest food in the gastrointestinal tract instead leak out into the surrounding tissue, causing significant inflammation and intense pain.

It's not unusual for an individual with pancreatitis to have recurrent episodes throughout their life. The pancreas produces enzymes that help digest fat and other substances in the gastrointestinal tract. In the case of pancreatitis, the enzymes leak out into the surrounding tissue in the belly and self-digest the body's fat stores and severely irritate the abdominal organs. Each bout of the disease is incredibly painful—on a scale comparable to passing a kidney stone—and requires treatment of supportive care to keep the patient well hydrated, control the associated pain, and ameliorate the secondary symptoms such as vomiting. During an intense flare-up, treatment can take as long as five to seven days and prove difficult in even the most compliant patient. A 300-pound Siberian tiger would certainly not be considered a very compliant patient, and Sasha was now a full-grown adult.

"JoAnne," I said, "thank you for getting me the blowpipe and the dart box."

JoAnne was a registered veterinary technician at the Franklin Park Zoo hospital, tantamount to a registered nurse, or RN, in human medicine, I first met her while working as a backup veterinarian for the two zoos in the Boston area: Stone Zoo, near my home in Stoneham, and Franklin Park Zoo in picturesque Olmstead Park, bordered by the communities of Dorchester and Brookline. I was on call for both zoos on my days off from my full-time job as a senior clinician at Angell Memorial Animal Hospital, so I had come to know JoAnne as a very experienced and competent veterinary technician who was also intimately familiar with the nuances of dealing with captive wildlife.

We were preparing to anesthetize, or "knock out," Sasha so we could provide the critically needed supportive care to help her through her current bout of active pancreatitis. I proceeded to prepare the dart. I made a habit of always loading my own darts with the appropriate amount of drugs, in this case, a combination of an anesthetic and a tranquilizer, ketamine and acepromazine respectively. A blow dart has two chambers: the forward chamber holding the drugs, and the rear chamber filled with compressed air. When the dart enters the skin, the cap on the end of the needle is pushed back exposing a hole on the side of the needle, which allows the compressed air to inject the drug into the animal.

Sasha usually resided at Stone Zoo, in a private suite complete with a swimming pool, where visitors loved to see the big cat up close—but not too close. The facility had been constructed especially for her when she was three years old. She had been confined for two years in Franklin Park Zoo's veterinary hospital for treatment of pancreatitis from when she was a cub, but when she had outgrown the facilities at Franklin Park, a $25,000 investment had been made to build her new quarters at Stone Zoo. However, since Sasha was having a particularly acute attack of pancreatitis, she had been temporarily transferred back to Franklin Park, where the housing and medical facilities were better equipped to facilitate proper treatment.

As Sasha had experienced this procedure many times in her life, in turn, it meant that whenever she saw the blowpipe or the veterinarian, she associated them both with receiving a shot and waking up with a headache, on top of already not feeling well. As one might imagine, this did not endear her to either the pipe or whomever she identified as the veterinarian.

I had never had occasion to tranquilize Sasha, so she didn't yet associate me with being one of the "bad guys." For this reason, I wanted to take great care in planning my first treatment session with her and possibly avoid such a tainted designation. So with my hopes high and the blowpipe in hand, I turned to John, the hospital ward attendant. He was a hard-working, dedicated individual who cared deeply for the animals he was responsible for. At the same time, John also needed clear, repetitive instructions on what was expected of him so he could carry out his tasks properly.

I said, "John, let's review everything again."

"Okay, Dr. Mark," John replied, "first I'll enter the barn and make sure Sasha is locked in the inside room. Then I'll distract her by unlocking the rings that operate the pulley systems used to open and close the door that separates her outside yard from the inside room. After that, you and JoAnne will enter the barn. You'll casually walk past me to access Sasha's yard from the outside while JoAnne is concealing the blowpipe so Sasha won't see it and get upset."

We each understood that once an animal like Sasha gets riled up, it's much harder to get a good shot and have the dart go where it should because she's so animated. Renowned for their immense power and strength, these majestic cats can jump as far as twenty-five feet forward, and vertically hop over a basketball hoop in stride. Also, if she became upset, her body would naturally release chemicals, such as adrenaline, that would be counterproductive to a successful tranquilization and treatment. So it would be imperative to minimize any noxious stimuli that might excite her, such as the blowpipe. Also along those lines, since Sasha and I had never met, my presence wouldn't be a cause for alarm either.

"Yes, that's right. Once you verify that Sasha's contained where she should be, JoAnne and I will go into the barn together. We'll then walk through to the outside yard, enter the tiger enclosure's outside compartment, and go stand by the door."

Inside the barn, Sasha was in an enclosure that had been retrofitted to be "tiger proof," meaning there was a floor-to-ceiling steel fence around the entire enclosure. Within the enclosure, a six-foot floor-to-ceiling metal door separated her indoor enclosure from the outside yard. The door would slide open and would close when operated by the pulley system.

"When you're situated with the pulleys, John, wait for my command before opening the door," I instructed. "Once I give the command, open the door, but only by one inch."

Opening the door a single inch while Sasha's attention was on John would allow me to slip the blowpipe through the small opening and shoot her in the rear quarter with the dart, without her knowing it was coming or who was doing the shooting. It was only about a seven-to-ten-foot shot, and I was quite good with a blowpipe. A perfect plan.

"Okay, Dr. Mark," John confirmed, "I got it."

With our scheme in place, John proceeded into the barn. In a few moments, John gave the signal that Sasha was contained in the right area, and I entered the barn with JoAnne. As we walked, JoAnne expertly smuggled the blowpipe by concealing it under her shirt and into her pants as she passed Sasha while the tiger's attention was focused on John unlocking the rings of the pulley system.

JoAnne and I made it to the door of Sasha's cage and stood next to it, safely separated from the big cat. We were all in position. Once I had the loaded blowpipe in hand, the next step was for me to give the command to John to open the door one inch. I turned to JoAnne and asked, "Are you ready?" She nodded her head affirmatively.

I positioned myself with the blowpipe ready to deliver the blow dart once the door was ajar. When all looked good, I gave the directive: "Open the door." On command, John opened the door, except he didn't open it just an inch, he opened it *all the way!* I gasped in shock and horror as my adrenaline kicked in at the sight of a tiger suddenly surprised at the sight of me with a blowpipe. I don't know for sure what a surprised Siberian tiger thinks, but I do know what it feels like to see one ten feet in front of you with no protective barrier. I can't begin to guess how many people have found themselves in this situation, but I'm fairly sure most of them are not around to talk about it.

This was not the introduction I had hoped and prepared for. My well-laid plans had gone awry. Not only was the introduction flubbed, but I was also suddenly in great danger with just ten feet separating me from 300-pound Sasha, who had over 1,000 pounds per square inch of crushing power in her jaw.

"Close the f**king door," I shouted as I simultaneously picked JoAnne off her feet and threw her to the back of the yard. In the brief confusion of the next fleeting moments, John realized what he'd done and quickly reacted by slamming the door shut. Luckily, it was just at the moment Sasha was recovering her senses, and her surprise was turning to violent aggravation.

With all my plans of covert operations summarily unmasked, a continued stealth mode was of no use anymore. I next loudly said to John, "Do you understand you are to open the door just one inch?"

"Yes," he affirmed.

Wasting no time, I quickly positioned myself with the blowpipe. "John, open the door *one inch.*" This time, he did open the door just one inch. I took the shot and successfully placed the dart in Sasha's hindquarter. When I saw her darted, I quickly withdrew the pipe and simultaneously ordered John to close the door. A few minutes later, the great tiger rumbled to the ground, and we went to work treating her pancreatitis.

John, realizing his mistake, could not find the words to say how sorry he was for the tremendous risk he had put us in. JoAnne and I were simply ecstatic we were able to hear his apology, especially given the possible alternative.

After a successful procedure, Sasha woke up, but, regrettably for me, I was forever imprinted in her mind as "one of those," a person never to be trusted again. From her perspective, all I would be good for now was shooting her with a dart and giving her a headache. I was disheartened but knew it to be true when weeks later after Sasha was moved back to her exhibit at Stone Zoo. It became crystal clear that in her mind, I was one of the deplorables. With most people, Sasha would exhibit playful behaviors, but when she saw me, the only interpretation for her behavior was that she wanted me for lunch to settle the score.

Fast forward a year later, and I was on rounds at Stone Zoo when one of the keepers asked, "Dr. Mark, can you please check Sasha and confirm if she's in heat?"

"Sure," I told the keeper, "I'll check on her and let you know if she's in oestrus." Oestrus is the recurrent period when the female is receptive to a male's sexual advances, which also coincides with when the female is ovulating and is commonly known as being "in heat." The two overlap to maximize the chances of pregnancy. When a female is in oestrus in the wild, they will vocalize and can be observed to be marking their territory with urine. Both of these behaviors will let a male tiger within the same territorial range know that a female is actively looking for a mate. In this way, tigers can find each other even though they tend to live and hunt by themselves.

Sasha lived by herself, which is normal for tigers as it is for other species of large predators, such as polar bears and great white sharks. In the wild, they only come together to breed. Although she lived alone in the zoo, Sasha had been implanted with birth control to prevent her from unnecessarily cycling. This was done for purposes of helping to prevent other medical problems as she matured. It had nevertheless been decided to remove her contraception implant because the zoo had chosen to introduce a male tiger into the exhibit with her. Zoo staff had removed Sasha's implant over two months before, ample time for the tiger to be in heat, so the keeper was looking for confirmation of whether she had started cycling again.

The introduction of a male tiger into an exhibit isn't only for purposes of breeding. Zoos are complex institutions, not immune to the pressures brought upon them by caring visitors who couldn't understand why Sasha was by herself. In reality, this was a false belief that any animal living by itself must be lonely. A zoo's goals include not only entertaining people but also educating them about wildlife and promoting conservation. So this factored into the decision to introduce another tiger to live in the exhibit.

Assuming the tigers' successful cohabitation, the zoo would display educational graphics to teach people that in nature, these animals usually live alone except when reproducing.

The best match for Sasha in this case, was her father, Boris, who was also living a solitary life. Neither tiger had any idea they were related, so to maximize the chance of success for them living together, zoo staff removed Sasha's implant, and she was allowed to cycle. This move was to take advantage of her natural behavior as a female tiger; Sasha would be more respectful and accepting of a male tiger if she was in heat. Since Boris had been previously vasectomized, there was no chance Sasha could get pregnant.

As I approached Sasha's enclosure, I was interested to see if she was exhibiting behaviors of being in oestrus, such as marking her territory, repeatedly lifting her tail as if to wave, or vocalizing. Such behaviors would normally let a male tiger within the same territorial range know that a female was actively looking for a mate. However, I certainly did not relish the thought of her less-than-welcoming behavior toward me, so I braced myself for the usual violent reception as I entered the hallway in the back of the exhibit.

From across the hall, Sasha saw me as I came in. I expected her to look at me as if I was the devil incarnate, the way she usually did. Instead, she turned around and lifted her tail as if to wave "come here, big boy," and purred.

I may have a healthy image of myself, but I have never thought of myself as looking or acting like a male tiger. Evidently, on that day, Sasha saw me through a completely different set of glasses. She thought of me as a male tiger, or at least to her a dominant figure, and for the first time since knowing her, she was receptive to my presence.

As for my report to the keepers, I could tell them that, without a doubt, Sasha was in heat. This was confirmed at a later date when I saw her out of heat, and she again wanted to make me the first course of her evening meal.

There are unique, difficult and often costly challenges in providing medical treatment to wildlife such that treatable problems are much more difficult to manage due to the nature of each species.

My interactions with Sasha reinforced that even though you love and respect a magnificent animal, to properly and humanely keep them in a captive environment requires creative methods combined with careful planning and extensive knowledge of their natural behaviors.

"Okay, open wide now and say, 'Ahhh!'"

Chapter 14

BETTY

"When are you going to have children?" my mother asked my beautiful wife Kris.

"I don't know," Kris answered with a mischievous twinkle in her eye, "We were thinking about having puppies instead."

This is not the answer a Jewish mother wants to hear to what she thought was a fair question. We had, after all, been married for a couple of years by then so my mother was not as amused as we were by Kris's response. Kris and I had been busy experiencing life together in our early marriage. We began our married life together in Boston. When I completed my internship at Angell Memorial Animal Hospital, I accepted a staff position at Andover Animal Hospital, thirty miles north of Boston, where we moved to live in a nearby apartment.

During my time off at Andover, Kris and I had the opportunity to sharpen our seafaring skills sailing a boat in the Caribbean. We fell in love with open water and felt our time on the sailboat was always heaven on earth. While in the Caribbean, we were delighted by an offer to stay in the home of Dr. Andy Williamson, a prior Angell Memorial intern, the only veterinarian with an animal clinic on the island of St. Thomas. In exchange, I would cover for him at his vet clinic while he was off the island away on vacation.

The arrangement went well and seemed a windfall when I was offered an opportunity to earn a year's salary working from March to October at an animal hospital on the coast of Massachusetts. Kris and I were excited at the prospects. The extra cash would allow us to spend half the year in New England and the winter months sailing down to the Caribbean and meandering through the islands. If we ever needed cash or a respite from living on the boat, Dr. Williamson would be happy to have me come by and help out at his clinic on St. Thomas. Everything was falling into place. I just needed to give the hospital a decision on their offer and begin what we thought was the perfect work-life balance.

In the midst of planning all of this, I received a phone call that changed the course of our lives. I got off the phone and said, "Kris, you're not going to believe this," I began. "Angell Memorial just offered me a job as a senior staff member at the hospital."

"What?" Kris said with surprise. "That's a phenomenal opportunity, Mark," she said, and then paused. "But what about living in paradise?" We had been entertaining thoughts of spending the upcoming year sailing along the New England coast, and down to the Caribbean, so this was a U-turn from our dreams of cruising adventures and a warm tropical winter.

"You're right, sweetie. We have a big decision to make." I felt it was an honor to be offered the position at Angell Memorial, a chance to work with some of the best veterinarians in the world. Kris also had more career opportunities as a physical therapist in Boston. However, we loved the idea of sailing adventures and the Caribbean lifestyle, so to put it mildly, Kris and I were torn. But then, life is full of curve balls.

In the course of the next few days, Kris threw out another

one—of a variety that would make my mother swoon with joy. "I'm pregnant," Kris said. "Well, I think I might be." The idea of a baby on the way in the midst of our other life-changing considerations caught us both off-guard. We had approached the possibility with an intellectual mode of "well if it happens, great," but we were in no way planning for it at the time.

Since this was before the advent of home pregnancy kits, we didn't know whether our—or I should say Kris's—intuition was correct. It was just weeks after Kris had joked to my mother that we were thinking of having puppies, so we found it somehow remarkable that we were unexpectedly visiting an obstetrician such a short time later.

"Kris and Mark, the test result is in," the doctor said. "I know this comes as a bit of a surprise, but still, I'm happy to let you know that, yes, you're pregnant. Congratulations." Hearing the doctor's announcement, we were instantly awash in an array of emotions oscillating between euphoria and abject fear. A spinning spectrum of life-changing images flashed before us—the late-night feedings, sleepless nights, projectile vomiting, dirty diapers—but we felt blessed by the new life we had created.

Our approach to life as individuals and a couple has always been to face everything very positively. As soon as I recovered from the shock of hearing the news, I looked at Kris and said with a gleaming ear-to-ear grin, "We are having a baby!"

It's possible for someone to feel overwhelming fear at the prospects of parenthood. For us, it was an exciting time that almost seemed like a fairytale. Kris and I were raised in loving homes by supportive parents. Perhaps it was because of our parents' positive examples, or the underlying confidence they had instilled in each of us, that instead of fear, we felt elation. We went to New York and told my parents in person. They were over the moon but, mysteriously, my mother was not surprised. Apparently, her mother's intuition had already informed her of our announcement.

The next phase of our lives began with us happily preparing for the arrival of our first child. And of course, this turned the tide on the job front, and I took the job at Angell Memorial. In doing so, we also decided to move closer to work to save time on commuting, so began house hunting.

After days of looking at several potential homes, we had a short list of favorites. We had some nice candidates on our list, but we hadn't found "the one," so we decided to take the time to look at one more house. It was in Stoneham, a suburb just north of Boston. It was smaller than the other ones we'd seen, only two bedrooms. When we went to look at it, the owner set us free to look around.

We made our way through the living room to the bedrooms and kitchen; the house was modest but cozy. "There's also a basement," the man informed us as we returned to the living area. "The door's just over there." As we made our way down the stairs, we found sunlight shining through highly unusual windows. We looked at each other smiling in astonishment and said, "We're home!"

As luck would have it, the people who owned the house were shipbuilders. The windows they had chosen for the dwelling underground were actually ship portholes. For us, coming down the stairs to the basement was more like descending below deck on a boat, a welcome reminder of our love of sailing and tropical adventures. That was the clincher; we didn't look at another house.

A few weeks later we moved into our new home, and although it was small, the house was perfect for us. In the backyard, we had an above-ground swimming pool and a garden for growing veggies. Beyond this, the backyard adjoined to miles of parkland in the Middlesex Fells Reservation area. We loved to enjoy the trails and natural habitats set amidst the hubbub of a busy metro region.

Also, just two blocks from our house was Stone Zoo. It was a very popular zoo of about twenty-six-acres set on the shores of the Spot Pond reservoir. Stone Zoo was home to a menagerie of exotic animals such as elephants, giraffes, zebras, pygmy hippopotami, flamingos, and a 1,200-pound polar bear named Major. Major had arrived at the zoo in July 1979, shortly after our wedding and instantly became the main attraction.

I couldn't have felt luckier. I was happily married to the love of my life and not only was I living my dream of being a veterinarian, but working at one of the most prestigious animal medical facilities in the world, Angell Memorial Animal Hospital.

Although I had a full-time position at Angell, I missed the challenge of working with captive wildlife, so on my time off I would act as a backup veterinarian to Dr. Bill Satterfield, the staff vet at both the Franklin Park and Stone Zoos. My responsibilities at the zoos came with the added perk of having 24/7 access to enter Stone Zoo at any time. Because our home was nearby, Kris and I got into a lovely routine of taking evening strolls through the zoo around sunset after the guests had disappeared.

We started each journey with a friendly hello to the sea lions, who would bark back at us, their sounds echoing throughout the area. As we passed through the peacocks' territory, the birds would fan out their magnificent feathers, strutting their stuff as they vocalized a signal that people were walking around their area. Similarly, the other animals took notice of our evening strolls through the zoo, having become accustomed to seeing us and acknowledged our presence in their own special ways.

No matter how many times I did this—either with Kris or in solo early morning walks—it was always a magical experience. At every turn was a flow of different habitats, ranging from the frigid Arctic to the sweltering tropics of Southeast Asia. A stroll at the zoo turned into a trip around the world—in only thirty to sixty minutes—depending on how fast we were walking—and with no passport necessary. I envisioned myself becoming part of whatever ecosystem or continent the animals in that area of the zoo were from. This simple exercise allowed me to feel as if I'd become one with the animals.

As the months passed, we continued our family visits to Stone Zoo, taking in the sights, sounds, and smells of animals from far-away lands. Some creatures were from places where the encroachment of human civilization on natural habitats had pushed their species close to extinction. In such cases, the animals were part of the zoo's breeding program for endangered species, such as exotic kudus and siamangs, and two orangutans from the jungles of Sumatra.

Sumatra is an extraordinarily beautiful Indonesian island known for its rugged tropical rainforests and smoldering volcanoes. Unfortunately, Sumatra has suffered a devastating rate of deforestation, putting in peril the future of orangutans, the world's largest tree-climbing mammal and Asia's only great ape.

Stone Zoo was fortunate enough to have two Sumatran orangutans, Betty and Stanley, both adult primates about twenty years old. On our evening rounds, Kris and I would often see the pair sitting quietly in their glass enclosures, looking like rusty-hued Buddhas.

Betty was accustomed to seeing us on our visits and would often come right up to the glass and greet us. Other times, we'd find Betty scrubbing walls like her keepers, using one of their brushes she grabbed. Betty was quite mischievous, often stealing their tools and then making them negotiate a trade of behavioral enrichment tools or food to get them back.

Betty had recently given birth. This had been her fourth pregnancy, but only one of the first three babies had survived. The zoo staff had been very excited to welcome the arrival of Betty's healthy newborn. Perhaps because of our own impending parenthood, Kris and I felt a special connection with Betty. As Kris's belly expanded, we watched in awe as the great ape mothered her newborn. Betty's maternal instincts were to be very protective of her baby, and so she kept it hidden between her arms and ample bosom. Because of this, we never actually saw much of the orangutan baby but still enjoyed seeing Betty caring so well for her youngster.

Not long afterward, we joined Betty in the realm of parenthood when I heard the words, "Mark! My water broke!"

It was 2:00 AM, and we had two couples staying over for the night. I was in the portholed basement, playing pinball with my cousin Richard. My knee-jerk response was, "Are you sure?" Obviously, this is one of the stupidest questions a man can ask—as any woman who has been in this situation can attest—and especially since Kris was at the top of the stairs, standing in a puddle. Her answer to my inane question consisted of mainly four-letter words—but I certainly deserved her wrath!

Just that morning, Kris had accompanied me to the New England Aquarium, where I had been called to care for a harbor seal sick with pneumonia. While I was tending to the animal, Kris started having Braxton Hicks contractions, named after John Braxton Hicks, the English doctor who first described them in 1872, and often called "false labor." Because I knew that such contractions could occur days, weeks, or even months in advance of delivery, I timed them as she walked up and down four flights of stairs in the building with me while I finished examining and treating the seal. As I'd listen to the seal's lungs, she'd tap me on the shoulder to let me know a contraction was coming.

Obviously, Kris's repetitive contractions signaled the actual beginning of labor—within hours, not days. As soon as I realized this after my ill-timed gaffe, I stopped playing pinball and, flew up the basement stairs, collected our packed bag and then hurriedly drove Kris to the hospital, leaving our house full of company behind.

Kris's labor was short. Within mere hours after arriving at the hospital, our daughter, Lauren-Emily, was born. Weighing eleven pounds and eight ounces, our beautiful little girl immediately captivated us as we counted her perfect ten tiny fingers and toes. We were overjoyed and grateful she was healthy, this wondrous miracle of our first child. Once we met Lauren-Emily, named for her great uncle and great-grandmother, who had passed away, our lives were changed for the good, forever!

Amazingly, the labor and birth happened so fast I made it back home in time to prepare breakfast for our guests sleeping over.

Soon, mother and baby were home to start life as a family. We settled into parenthood nicely, but with a new baby in the house, our trips to the zoo were on hold. It was early spring and still cold outside, so we didn't want to risk exposing our daughter to the elements. However, within a few weeks the weather started to warm, so we made plans to take Lauren-Emily out for her first trip to the zoo. A few days later, we bundled her up snug and safe and took our inaugural family walk in Stone Zoo.

As Kris and I made the rounds, it was wonderful to be there with our little girl for the first time. We checked in with each area, first saying hello to the sea lions and making introductions to the other animals we saw along the way. As our family troupe approached the region of tropical jungles, I thought of Betty. She was still very protective of her baby, so even though she was familiar with us, I expected her to remain very reserved in her maternal mode. What happened next was a total surprise.

Kris held our newborn baby at the big picture window of the exhibit, and then Betty approached them from inside the enclosure. She stopped for a moment, then suddenly opened her arms and held out her own youngster, presenting her to us. I was absolutely astounded. "Kris, do the same as Betty!" I urged. Kris held Lauren-Emily up to the windowpane.

It was a special moment in time for me—two mothers' eyes meeting across species lines in mutual support and approval, and their babies separated by just an inch of Plexiglas. I was totally captivated by this sight. It was a truly spiritual moment that filled our hearts and warmed the crisp air.

It was even more than that for Kris who, after looking into Betty's eyes that evening, felt a special kinship with her, never seeing her the same way again. I believe it's called a sisterhood. It's a feeling that has stayed with Kris all these years later.

I learned that day that one thing binds all life, and that's the miracle of birth, motherhood, and family.

Chapter 15

GIGI

The frenzy and fanfare around celebrity births have become commonplace these days, with social media and even traditional broadcasts announcing the sight of "baby bumps" and then counting down the days until the big day. Even animals have had their day in the limelight. Who can forget April, the giraffe in upstate New York, who had the world waiting, seemingly forever, for the birth of her baby? Long before all this, I attended to an animal celebrity mother-to-be—albeit without the immediacy of the internet—Gigi, the western lowland gorilla. As an example of how technology has profoundly changed the way we share awe-inspiring events like the birth of a gorilla, I was amazed that an Associated Press photographer could snap a picture in Boston and by using a new contraption called a fax machine, transmit the image to appear on the front page of a newspaper in Tokyo the next morning!

I was still working at Angell Memorial but was also "on loan" to the Stone Zoo and Franklin Park Zoo to cover for their full-time veterinarian, who had recently left. In reality, I had two full-time jobs, one at the hospital, the other at the zoos, but I was loving it! In addition to my regular day-to-day duties as the temporary vet, I was also asked to be the attending doctor to Gigi, a 220-pound western lowland gorilla who was expecting a second baby with her mate, Sam. There was a lot at stake, so I accepted the responsibilities on the condition that I'd be the person in charge since I would ultimately be the one held accountable. It was agreed, and I took on the oversight of a small team concerned with everything from prenatal to delivery and postpartum care.

I came onto the scene halfway through the pregnancy, a gestation period of about eight-and-a-half months, which made Gigi's due date December 25, 1982, Christmas day, and for me, it was just after Hanukkah. The impending birth during the holiday season made the event feel that much more special, like we were waiting for the arrival of our own special present.

The zoo had three adolescent gorillas: Gus, Kiki, and Quito. Gus came from the Bronx Zoo and Kiki, from the Philadelphia Zoo. Both had been rejected by their mothers and were on loan to receive our care and to keep the third baby, Quito, company. Quito was Gigi's baby, and she had also rejected him.

Dr. Deborah Schildkraut, a psychology professor at the University of Massachusetts Lowell and the Director of Research and Education for the Boston zoos, knew all too well the frequent occurrence of mother gorillas rejecting their babies. She explained the chain of events to me. Quito was the first gorilla born in Beantown, in June 1981. However, it became clear that Gigi wasn't caring for the infant and might even injure him so, at just twelve hours old, he was sent to live with a human foster family in Needham, a Boston suburb. The foster mother was an employee at the Boston Zoological Society and had been given leave to take on this responsibility. Deborah said, "Initially, the plan was for Quito to stay there for only six months, but it ended up being a year." For the family the year was full of newborn duties—bottle feedings, diaper changes, potty training—similar to raising their own children. "Quito came back to Stone Zoo a short time ago," Deborah said.

I asked, "Deborah, please remind me, how did Gigi react to Quito's birth?" Deborah managed the day-to-day behavioral needs of Gigi during her pregnancies and had worked with Gigi for five months before Quito was born, so she knew her well.

"Gigi seemed very confused during labor and delivery," she recounted. "Since she had no previous experience with infants or the birthing process, I believe she didn't know what to think or what to do when it happened. I think she was even frightened of the baby because she tried to stay away from him."

This familiar story in the zoo world came with an array of theories as to why, ranging from some mothers being too young when they gave birth to their having no maternal instinct or good role models. Compared to other animals, such as elephants and lions, which had been mainstays in menageries or zoological parks for centuries, gorillas living in captivity were a recent affair. Outside the jungles of Africa, gorillas were rumored mythical creatures to the developed Western world until their existence was confirmed in the mid-1800s. A century later, only a handful were found in zoos. With limited knowledge, most zoologists believed it would be impossible to breed gorillas outside their natural habitats.

This notion was famously dispelled on December 22, 1956, when a baby female gorilla named Colo came into the world at the Columbus Zoo in Ohio. Over a decade after Colo's birth, there were still less than twenty baby gorillas born in captivity, but the tide soon changed.

A hundred miles northeast of Colo's home in Columbus, the nation's second oldest zoological park, the Cincinnati Zoo, had a gorilla baby boom. The zoo boasted two pairs of procreating gorillas: King Tut, the gorilla patriarch of the park, and his mate

Penelope, along with Mahari, a female, and her partner, Hatari, who were all first-generation zoo inhabitants brought as young-sters from the wilds of Africa in the 1950s and 1960s.

Penelope, King Tut's partner, had spent the first three years of her life as a pet in the hospital-home of humanitarian Dr. Albert Schweitzer in French Equatorial Africa (today known as Gabon). While on a four-month excursion to Africa, the Cincinnati Zoo's veterinarian delivered a herd of Nubian milking goats and med-icines to the hospital, and, in return, Dr. Schweitzer presented Penelope to the doctor as a gesture of goodwill for the children of Cincinnati.

Both Penelope and Mahari had the distinction of simultane-ously kicking off the Cincinnati Zoo's gorilla population explosion. In learning the two were pregnant, the zoo implemented around-the-clock watches on closed-circuit televisions and a telephone hotline to the hospital with medical personnel standing by at the ready. Then, in January 1970, Gigi's mate, Sam, was born to Mahari, and days later Penelope gave birth to Gigi's older sister, Samantha. While Mahari took to cuddling her baby son, Penelope would have nothing to do with her daughter. Gigi was born two years after that, and it was the same story again when Penelope rejected her as well.

By the time Gigi and Sam were having the first gorillas born in Boston, the Cincinnati Zoo held the world's record for gorilla births with fifteen babies, 10 percent of the 150 gorillas born in captivity around the world, including the first gorilla conceived via artificial insemination and delivered at the Memphis Zoo in Tennessee. Although captive births were becoming less rare, pri-matologists were concerned about the low and possibly declining fertility of male gorillas as only 13 of 62 adult males in U.S. insti-tutions had sired children in recent years, and up to 50 percent were considered sterile.

While zoos were gradually cracking the code for gorillas to reproduce, from dietary considerations to the design of their enclosures, a gorilla mother who accepted and cared for their newborn was still a rare phenomenon. At the time, as many as 90 percent of infant gorillas born in captivity were rejected by their mothers, with the babies subsequently hand-raised by human caretakers. Some newborns were kept in "gorilla nurseries" in zoos or even hospitals, while others were cared for in people's homes, like Quito was with his foster family.

"I worked with Gigi for hours almost every day before Quito was born, trying to 'teach' her about mothering," Deborah said. "I wanted her to be comfortable with me around, so every morning I'd have coffee by her enclosure where she could see me and we could interact.

"I knew that for Gigi a baby would be something that was simply different, so I first tried to get her used to touching all kinds of things that were new to her. Once her fears reduced and she was used to that, I was concerned with how she would handle a delicate newborn, so I worked with her on touching something gently. When she did, I gave her a reward like grapes, one of her favorite treats."

"I remember. I was the backup vet then," I chimed in. "I also recall the baby gorilla doll you made for Gigi. It even made gorilla baby noises."

"Yes, but Gigi would have nothing to do with it," Deborah lamented. "As a mother myself, I wanted Gigi to experience the joys of parenting and bonding with her child. When that didn't happen, I somehow felt I let her down."

As a parent, I could relate to Deborah's sentiments. Even in moments when my daughter acted out or made a fuss, like children sometimes do, Kris and I always loved her and couldn't imagine our lives without her.

At the time, Stone Zoo was severely underfunded and, in many regards, antiquated compared to other zoos. In Cincinnati, gorillas moved out of their old-fashioned cages in 1978 to live as a troop in a new outdoor primate center, complete with tall waterfalls, swaying trees, and green grassy areas bounded by a fourteen-foot moat. Although Boston had a plan in place for years to build more modern enclosures, politics and lack of funding had delayed construction and remodeling efforts, so the great apes still lived in simple stone rooms with bars and glass windows.

Despite such challenges, the team at Stone Zoo felt twice blessed with Gigi being pregnant again and saw it as a second chance to try everything we could for her to have a successful birth and accept and rear the baby. This would include the ability for our team to monitor Gigi 24/7 to be able to watch for any signs of trouble. However, we would need special equipment that would allow us to observe her without causing more stress. Fortunately, after much searching, I was able to locate infrared cameras—which could record at night without lights—with the help of my brother Jeff. The used cameras, which came from New York, would have exceeded our budget but were graciously donated.

The team caring for Gigi's needs was purposely kept small, and consisted only of me, Deborah, and a few others who tended to her feeding and daily care. We were the only people allowed in Gigi's area—no reporters, no wealthy donors, political leaders, or curious zoo staff—no one was granted access unless they were a member of the working team. This not only helped to reduce the chances of triggering unnecessary anxiety but also served as further protection. In zoos, most human diseases are not contagious to the majority of animals because they're species-specific, especially ones that are viral, like a common cold or the measles. However, in the case of gorillas, whose species' genome is 98 percent identical to humans, diseases such as tuberculosis, measles, or the flu can cross species lines and in some cases be more virulent, so we wanted to minimize the chances of disease transmission.

While there was limited information on caring for and nurturing a mother gorilla and her infant, we were fortunate in that what knowledge did exist was openly shared between zoos in North America and around the world. Deborah turned over every rock and reached out to everyone who might have key learnings or an idea that could help. She even spoke to Dian Fossey, who at the time was a lecturing professor at Cornell University in Ithaca, New York. Fossey was the world's leading authority on mountain gorillas, famous for her extensive study researching the endangered species in their natural rainforest habitat in Rwanda, similar to Jane Goodall's work with chimpanzees. She understood natural gorilla behavior better than anyone, much of which she later documented in her autobiography *Gorillas in the Mist,* the bestselling book also adapted into a movie starring Sigourney Weaver.

"With the one-year-olds—Quito, Gus, and Kiki—in the enclosure next to Gigi," Deborah said, "I'm hoping she'll have a sense of being part of a troop, especially with Sam in the other enclosure as well. I also want her to see, hear, and smell young gorillas, so she's not scared by one when she gives birth. So far, I've been encouraged to see Gigi showing interest in them from her quarters."

Dian Fossey confirmed what Deborah and others working in zoos were learning. For gorillas, social structure was as important as food and water to the health and well-being of the gentle giants. Although we couldn't keep the great apes all together, given the limitations of the facilities at Stone Zoo, we could house them as neighbors. Because of Deborah's hard lobbying for structural changes at the zoo, Gigi would be able to observe the adolescent gorillas that would be next door receiving care on a daily basis.

"I'm also hoping that Gigi will see these little guys being cared for and be influenced by the example," Deborah went on. "Much like humans, gorillas learn by watching others. I think the more Gigi is exposed to the baby gorillas the better the chance she will recognize her baby as a gorilla and emulate maternal behavior, including to nurse it." As a veterinarian, I knew that besides the behavioral lessons for the infant, it was important for medical reasons that the baby drink milk from its mother to strengthen its immune system. This was another fallout of so many gorilla mothers rejecting their babies at birth. The newborns weren't getting their mother's colostrum, so they missed the benefit of the antibodies, which left them more vulnerable to infections.

It was a common practice in zoos to separate the father from the mother during pregnancy because keepers were fearful about infanticide since it happens in the wild. However, studies were showing that the longer the father stayed with the mother, the less likely the chance that would happen, so Sam and Gigi remained together until just weeks before the due date, when the team became concerned their roughhousing might injure the mother or unborn child. They could still see each other and communicate through the bars between their enclosures, including social signals between gorillas that occur through their odor emission and sense of smell in a form of olfactory communication.

Every decision the team made always had the best interest of Gigi and the baby in mind. So when we separated Sam from Gigi, we were careful to monitor them both for any signs of stress and, fortunately, we saw none. As Gigi's pregnancy progressed, all seemed to be on track and humming along.

Although things were going well, there was limited staff available to hold vigil during after-hours at the zoo, so Deborah formed

the "Gorilla Birth Watch," a cadre of volunteers made up of
zoo docents, or educated volunteer tour guides, and psychology
students from the University of Massachusetts. We were getting
close to the finish line, but couldn't be sure when it would come,
so for the last weeks of the pregnancy we had volunteers "man
the station" at all hours to report on anything that seemed amiss,
and, of course, ensure the big moment itself wasn't missed.

One night, in the wee hours of the morning, I was woken up by
a phone call from one of the student volunteers from the Gorilla
Birth Watch. She said, "Dr. Mark, it's happening!" I didn't need
to ask; I knew what it meant. Gigi was in labor. I roused myself
from sleep and was glad I lived just blocks from the zoo. In a
flash, I was out the door, rushing down the street with my heart
pounding and mind racing. I thought of Deborah and the team,
and all our hopes for Gigi and her baby now pinned on this cold
but clear evening, December 23, 1982.

Deborah and I arrived on the scene nervous as mother hens,
greeting the other team members and the volunteer lucky enough
to be there when Gigi went into labor. She felt like she'd won the
lottery—indeed, we all did, but we hoped that history didn't repeat
itself with Gigi. When Quito, was born, the new mother was so
disoriented that she inadvertently dragged the newborn around
the enclosure, endangering him, so the staff decided to remove
the infant to safer quarters. We had no way of knowing whether
all the hard work and prep this go round would have an effect on
Gigi, but we would soon find out when the baby emerged from
the womb, took a breath, and gave its first cry.

As the seconds ticked by, I looked at Deborah and crossed my
fingers in silence. It felt like an eternity, but within a few precious
moments, Gigi turned toward the sound of her baby's whimpering
and instead of running scared, she gently picked up the newborn

and cradled it in her arms. It was an amazing watershed event to behold, one forever etched in my mind.

With the baby accepted and safely in its mother's arms, Deborah and I stepped outside to the front viewing area for some coffee. With our cups in hand, we looked through the windowpane and smiled at the sight of Gigi nursing her newborn. It was a perfect holiday present. To say we were overjoyed was putting it mildly. By my side, Deborah gazed at Gigi, deeply touched by the joyful scene of bonding between mother and newborn, and by the knowledge that her professional hunches were right and all the hard work had paid off. She looked at me as if to exult, "I knew it! I knew it! I knew it!"

The national media had gotten wind of this story, and we had been holding the press at bay for months. They all wanted a sneak peek. We had allowed one lone photographer from the Associated Press to unobtrusively capture a few shots, which were transmitted via the wire service to newspapers around the globe. Television news crews had then followed suit and contacted the zoo looking to cover the story.

We didn't want a media circus but realized the coverage was an opportunity to tell our story nationwide. I had decided we should do it and allowed the first interview with NBC News, but in a very controlled way so as not to disturb the animals. "Further, any signs of distress and we'll need to stop immediately," I had told the producer and camera crew.

And so, I found myself looking into the lens of a camera in the front gorilla exhibit area doing a live national television interview. "I'm here at Stone Zoo in Boston with Dr. Mark Goldstein," the reporter began his intro standing by my side. "It seems we have a momentous occasion to celebrate this holiday season."

"Yes, we certainly do," I said with an ear-to-ear grin. The camera was rolling with a beautiful moment in frame behind me: Gigi protectively cradling her newborn. I felt like a proud papa. In front of me, but behind the camera, I saw Deborah beaming as well.

"Dr. Goldstein, why is this birth so important?" the inquisitive reporter asked as he held the microphone in my direction.

I thought of all the many reasons but made a simple reply. Television sound bites wouldn't accommodate such a long list of what it meant to Boston zoo institutions and their visitors, or improving the genetic diversity of the captive gorilla population, unlocking the reproductive mysteries of the great apes, or what it could mean to preserving the endangered gentle giants in the wild, an environment fraught with poachers and other human activities such as deforestation decimating their populations. Instead, I talked about why it was so critical that Gigi raise the baby, because no matter how well we might learn to rear the young of another species, the best chance for them to be healthy and well-adapted was to be reared by their natural parents.

"It's very exciting that Gigi accepted this baby. We know she rejected her first born, so what steps did you take to have this happen?"

The story of the gorilla toddlers and the team effort of talented people all rolled off my tongue. But as Deborah caught my eye in the background behind the cameraman, I was most appreciative of her never-ending devotion and patience in working with Gigi. The interview for NBC wrapped up, and we said our goodbyes to the television crew, then turned our attention back to caring for the gorillas.

The first days went well, although the team was perpetually nervous. We were on edge because even though Gigi was behaving normally in holding the baby close in her arms, it meant that all of our observations had to be from a distance. As a veterinarian, it's very unsettling to have to evaluate a one-day-old newborn hidden in its mother's powerful arms from twenty feet away. It was weeks before we were comfortable taking the necessary steps to examine the infant, but fortunately, all was well, and eventually, we knew Gigi's baby was a healthy male. The zoo held a naming contest, and the little ape became known as Kubandu, which means "gorilla" in the Limba language of West Africa.

Over the years, as Kubandu grew, the Boston zoos evolved as well, and so did my career. In 1987, I became the executive director of Boston's MetroParks Zoos, which included Stone Zoo and Franklin Park Zoo. We went from being one of the ten worst zoos in America—according to *Parade* magazine—to being fully accredited by the American Association of Zoological Parks and Aquariums in 1990.

Along the way, I had the privilege of continuing to work with Dr. Deborah Schildkraut, who never ceased to amaze me with her thoughtful ingenuity and profound sense of caring. Her seminal work with Gigi was a significant feather in Boston's cap for building a community of support for the zoos and constructing new and upgraded facilities.

Franklin Park Zoo's centerpiece of transformation was an exhibit over fifteen years in the making, the African Tropical Forest. I just loved the place. Its seventy-five-foot dome covering three acres of waterfalls, rocks, green foliage, caves, and gurgling streams was a wonderful new home for a wide variety of exotic animals, especially for six western lowland gorillas, including Gigi and Kubandu.

One of my favorite moments captured in the many press photos taken over the years, was on a warm spring day in the African Tropical Forest when Kubandu sweetly nuzzled his mother with a kiss. It always reminds me of my never-ending awe for the strong bond between a mother and her child, and the continuous need to foster that bond in humans and animals everywhere.

*Gigi looked like she was contemplating the future
for her baby, like all good mothers.*

Even though I was the person ultimately responsible for the decisions regarding Gigi's pregnancy and birth, I learned to listen, observe, and then act as a team. With the benefit of talented people like Deborah and the on-call obstetricians and pediatricians, along with the best practices shared by other zoos and gorilla experts, together we were successful. The value of teamwork was the most important lesson I learned from this experience and shared with the world that day.

Chapter 16

JOHARRE AND BABIRUSA

 **In December 1990, I accepted a position as** the director of the Los Angeles Zoo. My family and I left Boston in a blizzard and drove across the country, arriving in Burbank, California, to bright sunshine and swaying palm trees. Not long after I started, I was presented with one of those instances which a zoo director dreads. My day had started out with a scheduled weekly meeting of the animal curators, which I chaired. Here, each of the curators shared with the animal management group how their animals were faring. The updates gave an overview of the overall health, reproductive status, and management plans of each species in their care. We also discussed any exhibit and infrastructure changes that were in progress or needed repairs.

On this particular morning, we had a very animated discussion regarding whether to remove the birth implant in one of the chimpanzees to allow her to reproduce. Decisions like this are not made willy-nilly in a modern day zoological park. There are many considerations to factor, such as what impact the breeding, pregnancy, and an additional chimp would have on the overall health and well-being of the troupe. On top of this are additional costs and care that would be needed, as well as the various considerations of multiple departments weighing in, from development, marketing, and PR, to the education department concerned with how to build an educational component. Also taken into account is the impact on the overall captive population of chimpanzees in North American zoos, as there is an enormous amount of medical, genetic, nutritional, and behavioral science that comes into play with every planned birth at an accredited zoo.

At the end our meeting, I was just settling down to return some phone calls while eating my lunch when a distress call came over the radio: "Dr. Mark, chimpanzees have escaped their enclosure." What started as a typical day had suddenly turned into a crisis. "Do you copy, Dr. Mark?" the voice came again. "Chimpanzees have escaped their enclosure." These were the words that all zoo directors fear hearing.

"Yes. I'm on my way!" I said, trying not choke on the bite I had just taken as I jumped up from my chair. My office was on one end of the 118-acre zoo and the chimpanzee exhibit was on the other end. It was far enough away to consider taking time to find a golf cart, but under the circumstances and given my physical shape, I knew I could get there faster on foot than with a golf cart, so I took off running.

Part of my training as a veterinarian included learning that the first pulse you take when you walk into an emergency room is your own. You train yourself to become calmer as the circumstances deteriorate. This self-regulation is crucial because if the doctor becomes unhinged, everyone else does, too, and the patient suffers.

In this case, I had to remind myself first that I was the zoo director and not the veterinarian. As director, my job was to make sure that protocol was being followed and essentially stay out of the way. Of course, if something went wrong the buck stopped at my desk. This responsibility required me to observe what was happening in real time and only become involved if, and only if, the situation got out of control or an executive decision regarding the life of an animal had to be made.

Chimpanzees are surprisingly fast and are capable of running at speeds of up to twenty-five miles per hour—even faster than Usain Bolt, the fastest human sprinter in history. Although just three feet tall and weighing between 70 and 130 pounds, pound for pound, chimpanzees are incredibly strong and can easily overpower a person, which can make them extremely dangerous. With the potential for over a dozen chimpanzees of both sexes and all ages running free in the zoo, this would mean first securing the area to make sure the public was safe.

As I ran, I found calmness in hearing the reports come over the radio that our experienced keepers, excellent security personnel, and a capable veterinary staff were immediately going into action to implement our dangerous animal escape protocol. Along with securing the area, the veterinarian, in conjunction with the most senior curatorial staff member present, would also assess how many chimpanzees were out, where they were, and how they could be contained and then come up with a plan to return them to the exhibit. In these situations, deadly force is used only if a person's life is at risk. Nonetheless, there were personnel deployed with firearms to do so if necessary.

Out of breath, I reached the other side of the zoo and was welcomed by a cacophony of whooping and hollering. From atop the hill looking down on the chimpanzee exhibit, I was able to assess the extent of the situation. At first glance, the scene was actually quite funny. A dozen chimps were having a wonderful time dismantling the concession stand. They toppled soda machines and flicked pretzels through the air like Frisbees. They flung popcorn everywhere—a veritable blizzard of snack food. No wonder the chimps were making such a racket. They were having quite a party!

Fortunately, the concession staff and the public were safely out of harm's way. The chimpanzees were apparently contained in the concession stand area adjacent to their exhibit. The keepers were in sight developing a plan to lure the animals back into their enclosure, so it seemed things were under control.

My relief, however, changed to terror in a matter of seconds. Suddenly barreling my way, seemingly from out of nowhere, was the surreal sight of a mature male chimpanzee running down the path toward me. It was not just any chimp, but JoHarre, the dominant male of the troop. During my time working in Lion Country Safari Park while a college student, I had seen adolescent chimps pick up 500-pound pieces of petrified wood and swing them like baseball bats. I did not wish to be one of those bats, or for that matter, anything hit by one of those bats. Weighing in at over one hundred pounds, it would be nothing for JoHarre to completely dismantle me and in no time flat.

JoHarre was moving so fast that there was no time for me to take action and nothing, realistically, that I could do to stop him, so I simply stood still. Fortunately, my prayers were answered by the zookeeper in the sky, and JoHarre breezed on by me as if I wasn't there. I immediately got on the radio to let the staff know the situation. I knew the team would be focused on the chimpanzees at the concession stand and unaware of JoHarre's whereabouts.

It was not time to relax just yet. It was important to know JoHarre's whereabouts, so I took off after the big chimpanzee. I was neither capable of catching up to him, nor did I wish to since I had no way of restraining him, but knew I didn't want to lose sight of him. Ahead, I could see him weaving in and out among people who were just strolling through the zoo.

"What a great show this zoo puts on," I heard passersby saying.

"Get out of the way!" I shouted, realizing none of them understood the danger they were in. "Get out of the way!" I kept repeating.

Fortuitously, the planets must have been aligned, because the chimp paid no attention to the people he was passing, but we weren't out of the woods yet. JoHarre continued sprinting forward and quickly covered a quarter of a mile, then easily hopped a fence into the babirusa yard. The babirusa enclosure was on the periphery of the zoo, and was the last thing separating him from leaving the zoo grounds into the pristine Griffith Park golf course. At the zoo perimeter was a fourteen-foot-high fence, something JoHarre could effortlessly scale with one hand tied behind his back. I feared what might occur if that happened—but I knew it would not end well and we would be on the national news for all the wrong reasons.

As I chased him to the edge of the babirusa yard, I weighed the options, some of which could bring me into great danger. However, I still couldn't lose sight of the big male chimp, so I had no choice but to follow him into the babirusa enclosure.

Babirusas are in the pig family but don't at all resemble their domestic livestock relatives. Instead, babirusas look like a cross between a Dr. Seuss character and a dinosaur. Weighing as much as 200 hundred pounds, they are distinguished by their naked grey bodies and massive, spectacular curving tusks, which can reach lengths of seventeen inches. The tusks are, in truth, canine teeth, or fangs, that never stop growing. There are two sets of canines, with the lower teeth growing long to overlap the edge of the babirusa's snout, while the upper canines are truly magnificent. These teeth grow up and over the top of the snout, curving back toward the animal's forehead.

Babirusas are perfectly suited to living in the swamps and rain-forests of the remote Indonesian Islands, where their barrel-shaped bodies and deer-like legs enable them to maneuver easily through the dense vegetation and make them amazingly gifted swimmers. They've even been known to cross wide rivers and seas to reach other islands.

Since babirusas are from Indonesia and chimpanzees are strictly from Africa, the chances of them coming into contact in the wild are absolute zero. Even at the LA Zoo, normally there would be no logical reason for them to meet. Accredited zoos and aquariums in North America tend to exhibit animals often by their natural geographical distribution from around the globe, in part for maximizing both the recreational and educational value of every exhibit.

But today was not a usual day! I entered the yard but saw no sign of JoHarre or the babirusa. I moved on, and carefully turned the corner of a door to look into the barn where I suspected JoHarre had taken refuge. As I did, I couldn't believe my eyes. There was JoHarre, sitting back on his haunches, holding the tusks of the babirusa. They were just touching noses and staring into each other's eyes. I'm not suggesting it was love at first sight, but it was remarkably peaceful. They were just looking at each other.

After I remembered to breathe, I carefully backed out of the barn entrance and out of earshot of the unblinking pair of statues. "Ben," I reported over the radio to the veterinarian, "JoHarre is here in the babirusa barn."

"Okay," came the reply, "I'm heading your way."

I next snuck quietly back into the barn, needing to convince myself of what I had seen. As I looked around the corner, amazingly they were still sitting there as if frozen in time, peacefully looking at each other.

Within two minutes, Dr. Ben Gonzales' truck came cruising along the outer perimeter road of the zoo, contiguous with the fence of the babirusa yard, between it and a fence that was the last boundary before the golf course. Ben parked the truck and got out, carrying a blowpipe already prepared with a dart. He came over to me, but he was separated on the other side of a fence.

"I've got a good shot from here, Ben," I said. "Please pass me the blowpipe."

JoHarre was just through the open door of the barn, so I knew I could readily dart him from my position.

"Okay," Ben hesitated, and then respectfully continued, "I'll hand you the blowpipe, but if you successfully dart JoHarre, the likelihood of you exiting the barn before the sedative takes effect, and with your life intact, is zero."

I stopped for a moment and realized he was right. The induction phase could easily be anywhere from five to twenty minutes, during which time JoHarre would exit the barn and react to the bee sting that I had just delivered by handing me my head after first disassembling the rest of me. Adrenaline coursed through my body as I realized the colossal error I could have made. I returned to my senses and let the team secure the barn to restrain JoHarre safely and take him back to his exhibit.

The events surrounding the chimp "party" might sound humorous and somewhat exciting, given that no animal or person was hurt, and there was only the damage to the concession stand to deal with. But there was a sobering aspect of this frightening episode: The chimpanzees had been able to get out because, even though it was during open hours, a few misguided people had deliberately tied ropes to the railing and dropped them into the exhibit, providing the chimps with the ability to climb out of it. This "jail break" was created by animal rights activists who believe it is wrong to have the chimps living in captivity.

Unfortunately, their actions put both chimps and people at mortal risk. Having experienced firsthand the knowledge, love, energy, and forethought that staff members working with captive wildlife go to in caring for animals—often at their own peril—it is hard to reconcile such actions with the great danger presented both to people and to the magnificent animals for which that the activists purport to advocate.

When emotions run high, logic sometimes goes out the door. I'm forever grateful to Ben for being the voice of reason that day as he likely saved my life. The incident drove home the critical importance of being open to other ideas, and to think things through before taking action, especially when the stakes are high.

Ask Dr. Mark:

Why Do We Have Zoological Parks and Aquariums?

 Throughout my career, in each of my professional roles as a veterinarian, zoo director, and president of a progressive humane society, on many occasions people have asked me, "How do you feel about zoos and aquariums, or the concept of captive wildlife?"

I always offer the following caveat before providing the answer to the question: in a perfect world I wish we did not have them. However, we do not live in a perfect world. We live in an environment where, if I were a rhinoceros running wild on the plains of most African nations, the chances are catastrophically high that I will be hunted and slaughtered so my feet can be exported to serve as legs for a coffee table, or my horn can show up on an apothecary shelf in Asia. Given this reality, I would prefer to live in a well-managed, accredited humane zoological park in North America.

Throughout millennia, humans have taken animals from the wild and held them in captivity for a multitude of reasons, from the domestication of animals for food and beasts of burden to royal houses gifting them to other empires in a show of power, alliance, or servitude. From Egypt to China, throughout the ancient world rulers also kept menageries, or zoological gardens, for the viewing pleasure of the elite. In Rome, the empire notoriously captured and slaughtered millions of wild animals in the famous "beast hunts" of the Coliseum and other amphitheaters across Roman territories. In doing so, many species were devastated or even met with extinction, such as the Northern African elephant, not only by the demand for bloody entertainment but the encroachments of an exploding Roman population on natural habitats.

By the 1800s, private royal menageries gave way to zoological gardens made accessible to the public for entertainment and inspiration as well as for scientific endeavors. Modern-day zoos are institutions primarily inherited from this era, which over time have evolved as society at large has embraced more contemporary notions of ecology and environmentalism.

Like the ancient Romans, the advancement of "modern" civilization is deploying similar effects on wildlife populations and the environment, but on a massive global scale. For example, since 1900, the population of tigers roaming free in the wild has been decimated from 100,000 to less than 4,000, while countless other species have suffered the same fate, or worse. In a world where habitats and species are being destroyed at an alarming rate, accredited zoos and aquariums are bastions for animals on the brink of extinction, and a place for people to fall in love with them while learning about how important it is to save their habitats.

The term "accredited" refers to the American Association of Zoos and Aquariums accreditation process. In the past, I served on an accreditation team to evaluate a zoological park. I have also been the executive director of more than one zoological institution that went through the process of accreditation. I am in full support of the stringent requirements to be accredited, and the high priority placed on protecting and humanely caring for the animals for which zoos are stewards.

The professional staffs working at accredited zoos and aquariums continually develop new programs and protocols to enrich the lives of the individual species or animals entrusted to their care. In confining an animal in an exhibit or off-public holding area, a number of goals must be met. Along with reaching or surpassing all of the known nutritional and health needs, some basic and universal standards include ensuring that an animal lives as long as or longer than its wild counterpart. Further, they should not develop any disorders or diseases not seen in the wild or develop harmful or unnatural behaviors, such as self-mutilation, continuous pacing, or other abnormal repetitive or destructive behaviors.

Just as important, the animals should be able to reproduce genetically sound, physically and behaviorally healthy offspring. The ability to do so when provided the opportunity and accompanied by a well-thought-out breeding program helps support the goal that all the needs of that species are being met.

Accredited zoos and aquariums all over North America contribute invaluable scientific information to advance our knowledge and understanding of the species that run and jump and crawl and fly and swim and burrow across our earth. This intelligence contributes not only to improving the captive population's care but also to saving their counterparts in the wild.

In working with a captive population of a species intended to be released back into the wild, zoo professionals go to extraordinary lengths to not allow the animals to imprint on people. At the same time, they provide ample opportunity for the animal to learn to be self-sufficient and develop the natural behavior patterns of that species. Along with caring for species on the brink of extinction and reintroducing them back into the wild, institutions have countless programs going on geared toward stemming the tide of extinction, some of which I highlight in stories in this book.

With an awareness that we live in a real world that threatens the well-being and future existence of many species of wildlife, I have come to believe in the wisdom of Baba Dioum, a Senegalese poet and environmentalist:

In the end we will conserve only what we love,
we will love only what we understand,
and we will understand only what we are taught.

As part of having hope and working to reverse the damage to wildlife populations and habitats, along with the scientific contributions on those fronts, I believe we need accredited zoos and aquariums to help educate the generations of today and tomorrow. Because when we love something, we protect it.

An example today is the work being done at San Diego Zoo Global to preserve the northern white rhinoceros. There is no longer a living male northern white rhinoceros left on the planet, making them critically close to joining the long list of mammal species that have gone extinct since 1900.

At the beginning of the twentieth century, over a million rhinoceroses were roaming Africa's savannas and Asia's tropical forests. But much like the fate of the American bison, or buffalo, in the Midwestern region of the United States and Canada, rhinoceros populations were first decimated by widespread sports hunting around the turn of the century. This was followed by a rapid loss of habitat as industrial agriculture cleared vast swaths of land to plant crops, and, in turn, the human population exploded.

Further devastation continued for rhinos as the victims of large-scale poaching, driven in part by the growing demand in Asia for powdered rhino horn used for various medicinal purposes. Such poaching began in earnest when China's Chairman Mao Zedong called for the use of traditional Chinese medicine over Western medicine start-ing in the 1950s. In the case of the western black rhino, this resulted in an astounding 98 percent reduction in popu-lation by 1995 and their extinction a short decade later.

Such human industry has driven the entire rhinoceros species dangerously close to extinction. With many sub-species already gone, the northern white rhinos are the latest on the brink. The case of the rhinoceros is simply a case in point for the fate of all living things. Some scientists now say such overall planetary phenomena may have the whole of Earth on the brink of its sixth mass extinction, the first since the lost era of the great dinosaurs.

While there are many broad-scale issues we humans would be wise to address sooner than later, currently, in the case of the northern white rhino, some hope comes in the form of semen collected and preserved from the species' last male before he died in Africa.

San Diego Zoo Global has plans to use this semen for in vitro fertilization, which is combining semen and an egg in the laboratory, in working to bring the northern white rhino back from what seemed certain extinction. Eggs har-vested from one of the only two remaining northern white rhinoceros females, both living on the Ol Pejeta Conser-vancy in Kenya, will be inseminated in vitro with the semen of the deceased northern white rhino male, resulting in a viable northern white rhinoceros embryo. To lower the risk to the only remaining females, the embryo will be safely implanted in a surrogate, a southern white rhinoceros. The resulting calf will have the DNA of a northern white rhino, effectively reversing extinction of the species.

We can find other hopeful endeavors today in vast collections of semen, eggs, and tissue samples that have been cryogenically frozen in massive ark repositories, such as in the American Museum of Natural History's Cryo Collection in New York City, the Smithsonian Institution in Washington, DC, and the Frozen Zoo at San Diego Zoo Global. Along with these genetic repositories are large-scale undertakings to study molecular evolution via the Genome 10K Project, which is working to sequence 10,000 genes from 17,000 species to study molecular evolution. Or the International Barcode of Life project, a consortium of repositories intent on creating 5 million barcode records from the DNA of a half million species.

Chapter 17

SAM AND THE RHINOS

 My life work has put me in many unique situ-ations that most people would never dream of finding themselves doing. One minute I could be crunching numbers for a budget and the next collecting semen from a rhinoceros or a gorilla.

The first time I met Dr. Stephen Seager was between my third and fourth year of veterinary school at Cornell. That summer, I was lucky enough to work at the National Zoo in Washington, DC. Along with being able to work with Dr. Seager, I was also fortunate to work with another leader of modern zoological medicine, Dr. Mitch Bush, who pioneered such important clinical innovations as safe anesthesia techniques for captive and free-roaming wildlife.

Like many of the jobs I had during my youth, I had gotten the position simply by being gutsy and asking. "Mark," said Dr. Bush, "why don't you take a day and come with us to help Dr. Seager on a special project. You'll learn a lot." I considered Dr. Bush a mentor, so took his advice even though I didn't really know what I was getting myself into.

Less than a decade before, Dr. Seager had come from his homeland in Ireland to join the faculty of the University of Oregon Medical School, where he produced the world's first live litter of normal healthy puppies from frozen semen in 1969. He was a trailblazer at the leading edge of trends in the scientific community. His visionary mind saw that extracting and preserving semen from endangered species could be a major step forward in reducing the rate of extinction. Such frozen semen could be used to inseminate females of the same species, some of which may be thousands of miles away from the male, making direct copulation impossible. It could also be used in research or other reproduction methods, such as fertilizing extracted eggs in a laboratory and then implanting the embryo in a surrogate uterus.

At the time I found myself at a safari park in 1977 standing next to a rhinoceros in a squeeze cage, there were only a few researchers and institutions beginning to collect and freeze genetic material.

When I met Dr. Seager then, he was at the forefront of semen preservation, having already collected samples from seventy-two species of animals, including camels, leopards, gorillas, and elephants, many of which were endangered. As part of this work, he had come to the safari park to collect semen from twenty-one endangered white rhinos.

The rhinos lived in Lion Country Safari, where 300 wild animals roamed freely across 120 acres on the eastern side of the Kings Dominion Family Entertainment Center in Doswell, Virginia. From the safety of a monorail train, visitors could catch a close-up glimpse of lion prides and herds of giraffes, elephants, antelope, and a menagerie of other wildlife, along with enjoying the towering roller coasters and other amusement park fare.

Since Kings Dominion is just an hour south of Washington,

DC, I had previously spent time at the safari park working on various veterinary tasks, but I had never done anything like this. With rhinos, my experience had been in examining or treating them, but this was quite different—I mean, you didn't just go up to a 4,000-pound male rhinoceros and ask him to fill a cup with semen!

This procedure would take a lot of planning, patience, and careful execution. And in this case, it would also take electro ejaculation. Electro ejaculation is the application of electrical stimulation to the sexual organs to retrieve semen. By gradually increasing or pulsing electrical current delivered through a probe, which in the case of a rhinoceros resembled a small torpedo with wires on the end, correctly inserted into the rectum, a technician can induce the appropriate glands to contract and expel semen in ejaculation. This method had been used since the 1930s as a tool for breeding farm livestock such as cattle.

From my training at Cornell, I had some knowledge of artificial insemination methods used with domestic animals, but the techniques and equipment employed with large wild animals were all new to me. At best, I was certain the electro ejaculation of a rhinoceros would be difficult to perform, and at worst, dangerous.

However, Dr. Seager had pioneered electro ejaculation techniques for use in wildlife insemination, learning as he went and then applying his discoveries to various species of animals. In the 1980s, he also went on to apply the same technology to neurologically impaired men. In fact, through his training of physicians around the world in the use of electro ejaculation, approximately 40,000 children have been fathered by men with spinal cord injuries or other neurological disorders who may not have otherwise produced children.

"Okay Mark," Dr. Seager said, "Dr. Bush indicates the rhino's darted."

The two-ton beast started to stagger, but he was safely standing in a squeeze cage, a chute enclosure designed for humanely
restraining large animals. The chute was fitted with walls of thick
steel pipes, heavy duty enough to withstand the brute force of a
rhino, and massive doors at each end on rollers and tracks that
could be opened and closed quickly to move the rhinos in and
out. Restraining the rhinoceros in the squeeze cage would allow
the animal to remain in an upright position even while under a
sedated state of "twilight" semi-consciousness and still achieve
ejaculation.

The squeeze cage was at the end of a chute leading in from a
stockyard that looked like a battlefield of four-legged skirmishing
tanks. Fortunately, no combat was underway, just minor clouds
of dust as the large animals moved around or into the chute at
the behest of their keepers.

I've always been amazed at the skills of captive wild animal
keepers. They're the counterpart to a horse or dog "whisperer,"
knowing the patterns of each species with an almost Dr. Doolittle
sense that allows them to use behavior in the control of an animal.
For instance, they know that a rope around the snout will cause
swine to pull back, whereas a carnivore will be more likely to
attack. Similarly, a rhino can't be handled like a cow or a horse.
Doing so can quickly get someone injured or killed. Staying alive
and keeping the animals safe requires knowing the animals and
using your brains and not your brawn to work with them.

When one herds large animals such as rhinos in Africa, simple
tarps are often made into chutes used to move them in a particular direction. The animals don't know it's only a tarp they could
easily barge through; they just see it as a visual barrier. Similarly,
the keepers at Kings Dominion herded the rhinos into the stockyard and then coaxed them one at a time down the chute to the

squeeze cage, where the team for the procedures was waiting out of sight from the herd.

We remained hidden to reduce any agitation the rhinos might experience in seeing a stranger in the stockyard area. It was important to keep the animals as calm as possible throughout the procedures to ensure the rhinos' safety and the safety of those working with them.

"He's nicely sedated now," said Dr. Seager. "We can get started."

The rhino's keepers had worked their magic in the stockyard; now it was our turn to collect the semen. Dr. Seager began by slowly inserting the rectal probe, a phallic-looking object with two wires connected to it and a sophisticated transformer. The rhino remained calm as Dr. Seager continued to place the probe skillfully at the right depth, and once he was satisfied it was in the proper position then turned to the transformer equipment.

"Okay, Mark, I'm going to start stimulating the sexual organs with a low-dose electric charge."

I positioned myself near the rear underside of the rhino. After a few minutes the penis, which normally curved backward to allow urination for territorial marking, enlarged until fully erect and extended over two feet forward, being shaped somewhat like a lightning bolt. As I'd spent a lot of time working in safari parks, this wasn't the first time I'd seen a rhino with an erection, but I'd certainly never purposely approached one. So even as a vet student, I was nervous about successfully performing the task at hand.

"It's about that time," Dr. Seager indicated as he was tracking the progress.

With one gloved hand, I retracted the prepuce, or protective foreskin, and exposed the penis. In the other hand, I held a collection cup at the ready. At the same time, I tried to gauge the "when and where" of how best to catch the sample as the rhino, and even the wind, moved the target around. Compounding this unwieldy feat further was the need to prevent contamination of the sample, which meant the cup couldn't touch the rhino.

I took a breath and focused until the singular moment finally came, then reached out the cup like a catcher's mitt and somehow caught the first sample. All things considered, I sighed a breath of relief at my beginner's luck. "Nice job, Mark," Dr. Seager cracked. "That's one down and twenty to go!" By the end of the day and twenty-one rhinos later, to say the least, I was very familiar with Dr. Seager and his methods of working. Indeed, there were probably more people who had gone into space than could put on their resume that they've helped ejaculate a rhinoceros.

Years later, I was working as the director and CEO of the MetroParks Zoo in Boston, with oversight for both the Franklin Park Zoo and Stone Zoo. Given my managerial duties, and the zoos having their own full-time veterinary and curatorial staff, I didn't perform any clinical work day to day and hadn't since leaving Angell Memorial Animal Hospital when I took the position to head up the zoos in the late 1980s.

During my tenure there, Dr. Seager came to Boston specifically to collect semen from our male western lowland gorilla Sam. Gorillas are the largest of the great apes. Native to the Congo Basin, the western lowland gorillas are the smallest and least endangered of the gorillas, but like other endangered species, these magnificent animals have seen their populations devastated by habitat destruction as well as poaching and disease.

However, since I had worked with Dr. Seager on similar procedures a decade before, he knew I was familiar with the protocols and his way of doing things, I was not surprised that he asked that I assist with the procedure. Further, Dr. Jack Curtin, the zoo's veterinarian, understood the request for me to assist, so I capitulated and agreed to help.

Responding to the rapid, permanent loss of endangered species around the world, in 1981 the Association of Zoos and Aquariums launched the Species Survival Plan (SSP), a population management and conservation program to help ensure the survival of select endangered wildlife species into the future. The SSP programs are meant to provide a link between zoo animals and the conservation of their wild counterparts through cooperative scientific breeding programs, education, research, habitat preservation, and, in some situations, in returning animals to the wild.

Sam had been born to parents Hatari and Mahari, as the first lowland gorilla birth at the Cincinnati Zoo in 1970. At eighteen months old, when diagnosed with a serious blood disease, his father Hatari donated blood in the world's first gorilla blood transfusion that saved the youngster's life. Sam also had epilepsy as a youth, but as is sometimes the case in humans, the young gorilla outgrew the condition as he got older.

When Sam was nine years old, he and a gorilla named Gigi, the pair having been deemed incompatible with the other gorillas in Cincinnati, were sold at a charity auction to a Golden Gloves boxing champ. It should be noted that auctions regarding any endangered animal in North America have been obsolete now for decades. Today, endangered animals are moved or loaned to various accredited zoological institutions based on what is best for a species as a whole. The Species Survival Plan group for the species in question guides these decisions.

The boxer was Peter Fuller, a man who, in 1977, thirty years after winning his Golden Gloves title, dared to step into the ring with Muhammad Ali to raise money for a charitable cause through a series of short boxing bouts. Fuller was the son of one of the wealthiest men in America, Alvan Fuller, owner of Boston's first auto dealerships and governor of Massachusetts in the 1920s. At their Runnymede Farm in North Hampton, New Hampshire, Fuller bred and raced thoroughbred horses, including horse racing legend, Dancer's Image, who in 1968 rallied from last place to win the Kentucky Derby, and then three days later was disqualified in a highly controversial decision revolving around doping. In addition to racehorses, Fuller had an affinity for gorillas. He became a staunch supporter and driving force behind the gorilla program at the Boston zoos and donated Sam and Gigi to Stone Zoo, where the pair lived and produced two offspring.

In the captive gorilla population in North America, Sam's lineage was not significantly represented, making his semen very valuable to ensure healthy genetic variation.

In the procedures with the rhinos, I was nervous because of my inexperience. Now I felt nervous because, in my director position of the zoos, it had been awhile since I'd rolled up my sleeves doing clinical work. Most of my staff knew me as an administrator, not a clinician. Also, ejaculation methods vary for each species, so this procedure would in some ways be different from the one with the rhinos.

Since there was a lot at stake with this procedure, Dr. Seager wanted to get a good sample without having to come back and do it another day or to expose Sam to further sedation. So for those reasons, he requested my assistance.

"All right, everyone," Dr. Seager directed the attention in the room, "before we get started, let's review the plan once more."

There was a large team, including Dr. Seager and me, plus four others who would each be responsible for holding an arm or leg of the gorilla while he was under sedation, as well as someone to archive the important and rare procedure so others could later piggyback on our success. Sam would be lying on a stainless steel table and unable to stand. Also on hand would be a few other keepers and medical staff who would be observing, as well as someone with a camera to archive the important and rare procedure.

Weighing in at over 400 pounds, Sam was incredibly strong. Although not a vicious animal, with his immense power he had severely injured and broken both hands of his keeper. The keeper had violated protocol by extending her hands into the exhibit to feed Sam and he unexpectedly grabbed her and tried to pull her into the exhibit. Gorillas are not typically aggressive, but in this case it was hypothesized that because the keeper was having her menstrual cycle, his response may not have been one of aggression but a miscalculation.

"We all know the importance of keeping Sam's limbs under control," Dr. Seager instructed. "If a keeper were to lose their grip, Sam, even while under sedation, could easily and with incredible force swing a leg or arm awkwardly in any direction. For anyone who happened to be in the way of one of those swings, it would be like getting kicked or punched by a super-sized professional fighter, likely landing them on the other side of the room with someone dialing 911. That's not a call any of us wants to make."

"Dr. Mark, after Sam's sedated, I'll get the electro ejaculation probe in place. Then your role will be to collect the semen specimen."

To obtain the sample, Sam's penis would need to be exposed while a receptacle cup was at the ready to make the collection. However, different from collecting semen from a rhinoceros, a gorilla's penis must also be stroked. No matter the importance of the stakes, or even it being a clinical setting, there's just no getting around that these situations can sometimes feel awkward. But we were there to do a job, so any such feelings were put aside as the team went about the business of sedating Sam and positioning him on the table.

Dr. Seager placed the probe into the rectum to the appropriate depth. In his state of sedation, Sam had no response to the intrusion. Dr. Seager then stepped to the side to use the transformer. As he did, I situated myself between Sam's outstretched legs, each held by one of the keepers. The electrical charge would stimulate other muscles in the area to contract in addition to the sexual organs, so I was keenly aware that if any one of the four people holding the limbs lost control, I could be seriously injured. Fortunately, no such outbreaks occurred, and we were successful in collecting the semen.

In the next instant, I knew my director status had somehow changed forever when one of the staff said, "Nobody can say that Dr. Mark isn't a *hands-on* manager."

The proverbial elephant in the room dissipated in a round of chuckles as someone else chimed in with "Yeah, he's got the right touch."

Sam ultimately woke from his sedation oblivious to the awkward situation—one that doesn't usually qualify for polite dinner conversation or something to put on a dating website—while everyone blew off steam with some humor.

What I didn't originally factor into my willingness to assist was that the staff would respect me for getting into the trenches. It was a learning moment for me and cemented my management style throughout my career.

Today, I have enormous respect and gratitude for pioneers such as Dr. Stephen Seager and Dr. Mitchell Busch. Their work and dedication have shown the tremendous value that technological advancements and science can play in stopping and even reversing the extinction of the amazing animals of planet Earth.

I shared this story with my good friend Josh several years later, and he immediately remarked that he would never look at me the same way again. He claims he has great respect for what I do, but for some reason, he never shakes my hand.

Chapter 18

MRS. HARPST

As the saying goes, "It takes a village to raise a child." Likewise, animal welfare organizations are dependent upon dedicated people in the community to rescue abused and abandoned animals, and they need to raise funds to provide for their shelter and care. This work is not for the faint of heart and these nonprofit entities are constantly in need of financial support.

In February 2001, I had taken the position as president of the San Diego Humane Society and SPCA (SDHS), enticed by the organization's board leadership and multimillion-dollar vision for upgrading and expanding their facilities and programs to encourage more adoptions and expand their educational programs. I was thrilled. I believed in the vision of the SDHS board and jumped at the opportunity to utilize my experience as a veterinarian, my expertise in animal welfare issues, and experience as an executive administrator, to do something significant in support of the human-animal bond in San Diego.

Established in 1880, SDHS was one of the earliest humane societies in the country and the oldest continuous running nonprofit in San Diego County. In the 1970s, the SDHS formed the Animal Rescue Reserve (ARR), a group primarily staffed by volunteers trained to be first responders during disasters, who became the model for other animal welfare agencies to emulate nationwide. Since then, SDHS had earned a reputation for being on the leading edge of techniques and practices in animal welfare, but the shelter's housing in a former milk plant on Sherman Street since the 1950s limited their capabilities.

SDHS had offered me the job three years before, but we hadn't come to terms. Instead, I went to work as senior vice president for the progressive San Francisco SPCA, an organization known to lead the way for many groundbreaking trends in animal welfare, including the movement to eradicate euthanizing adoptable animals in shelters and the Maddie's Pet Adoption Center, which opened in 1998.

The humane society in San Diego was making plans to develop a joint property with the county and consulted with SF SPCA to learn from their experience incorporating their revolutionary design of sheltering dogs and cats in cozy, homelike settings rather than cages. Our concept was not only to upgrade and expand the SDHS facilities but also to cooperate more closely with the county in a common area.

One of my primary responsibilities at nonprofit SDHS was to raise funds. I saw promise in the San Diego donor base, but being the newbie on the block, I didn't have my own ready-made list of contacts, so I had a lot of work to do.

While at my desk in the evening, I came across a plain four-by-six-inch envelope, the kind of modest stationery readily found at a local discount store to use for a quick note. It was hand addressed to "Dr. Mark Goldstein, President of the San Diego Humane Society," but there was no return address. I was new on the job and not well-known in the area, so I was surprised to see mail specifically sent to me. The handwriting on the envelope caught my eye because it was carefully crafted, harking to bygone days of letters carefully composed, when the aesthetic beauty of scribing the written word was appreciated. I therefore suspected it was penned by an elderly woman, and I somehow felt connected to the sender.

After opening the envelope and removing its contents, I was surprised to find a handwritten note on a small piece of blank notepaper along with a check made out to the "San Diego Humane Society" in the amount of $250,000. The annual operating budget of SDHS at the time was $4.2 million, which meant this check represented over 5 percent of the entire budget.

Cautiously excited, I called Shelly Stuart, our director of development. "Hello, Shelly," I said when she picked up the phone. "I'm sorry to call when you might be on your way out the door, but I need to ask you about something I just found in the mail." It was almost dinnertime, and I always tried to respect my staff's personal time but this was not an ordinary moment. True to her nature, Shelly was still hard at work in her office. I explained what I had found and asked if she might know anything about it.

"Yes, Dr. Mark. That's very real!" she said with giddiness in her voice. "I'll be right down to explain."

In my experience, many donors who made major contributions would have strings attached or want something in particular, so I was interested to hear what our benefactor might have in mind.

Shelly entered my office with a smile. "Dr. Mark, for the past few years, like clockwork each March, we receive a check from a woman who lives in Coronado. The first check was for $100,000, and the amount has increased every year since." I waited for Shelly to explain any conditions associated with the donation, but she continued with the story. "The first time a check arrived I got a call from an attorney who said she represented the donor, Mrs.

Frances Harpst. She told me the check was real but made it crystal clear that under no circumstances did Mrs. Harpst wish to be contacted in any way."

I was astonished. By this time in my career, I had significant experience with fundraising, and I had never gotten, nor heard of anyone receiving, this amount of money in such a modest manner. My experience was just the opposite with large money donors; most would want the facility in their name or some other such recognition.

"I'd like to send Mrs. Harpst a thank you at least," I said.

"No, Dr. Mark, you mustn't," Shelly said adamantly. "The lawyer was very definitive that any attempt to contact Mrs. Harpst, even to say thank you, would jeopardize future support."

My astonishment turned to wonder as I handed Shelly the check. "Okay," I capitulated, "we'll accept her generous gift and respect her wishes."

As the years ticked by, each March a check would unceremoniously arrive in the mail. Every time one appeared, I'd marvel and wonder about the nature of the woman behind the magnanimous gesture. This went on in seeming perpetuity until one March nothing arrived from Mrs. Harpst. I became worried something may have happened to her, so against the direct order to never contact her, I mailed a simple handwritten note to see if she was okay.

Not long afterward, I received an envelope in the mail addressed to me in Mrs. Harpst's unmistakable handwriting. I stared at it apprehensively, afraid I had overstepped my bounds or offended her. I knew little about Mrs. Harpst, but I heard she could be a curmudgeon, not shy to speak her mind, even gruffly so. With trepidation, I opened the envelope and read the note. To my relief, instead of telling me to get lost, Mrs. Harpst thanked me for inquiring about her well-being and apologized for her tardiness in sending the check for SDHS because she'd been ill. I then noticed the check amount. To my amazement, Mrs. Harpst had increased her donation!

After that, the annual arrival of checks returned to their regular schedule until a few years later. In 2010, SDHS was contacted with the sad news that Mrs. Harpst had passed away. In hearing of her death, I felt I'd lost a sort of distant pen pal, someone I'd never met, but with whom I felt an association through a shared love of animals. I attended the funeral out of respect and gratitude for her generous support of SDHS. It was only after she was gone that I learned more about the woman who quietly supported our efforts to make a lasting mark in the community and improve the lives of animals.

Frances "Fran" Harpst was born in 1926. Her father, John Fish Goodrich, was one of the most popular screenwriters in Hollywood until he unexpectedly died of complications following surgery when his daughter was just ten years old. Fran's mother, Frances Nunnally, was born into the upper crust of Southern aristocracy in Atlanta, Georgia, heiress to a fortune made when Fran's grandfather helped finance a buyout of the Coca-Cola Company in 1919.

As a young girl, Fran fell in love with Coronado Island while summering with her mother at the iconic Hotel del Coronado, a relaxed setting of seaside charms just minutes from downtown San Diego. She later met her husband, Walter "Wally" Harpst, at the hotel while he was playing a gig as a musician. The marriage didn't last, but Fran made Coronado her home and soon became an active community member, serving many local causes and founding the Meals on Wheels program in Coronado.

Fran continued a legacy of philanthropy handed down from her mother and grandmother, Cora, also a lifelong animal lover.

Cora was an accomplished equestrian who broke her back in an unfortunate riding accident so began raising champion Afghan and whippet dogs. She supported animal causes throughout her life, but like her granddaughter, shied away from recognition and attention for it.

Fran may have had a rough exterior at times, but underneath was a heart of gold. She generously donated time and money to support her love of animals in the tradition of her mother and grandmother. We at SDHS felt incredibly blessed by Fran's support for so many years and were saddened to hear of her loss, yet she had one more astonishing surprise for us.

"Dr. Mark," Shelly said, "here are the details of Mrs. Harpst's estate." Reviewing the documents made my jaw drop. In her last act of benevolence to SDHS, Mrs. Harpst left us an astounding $20 million! I reminisced back to the first check that had shown up on my desk so many years before and thought *what a wonderful world.*

I'll never know the reasons Mrs. Harpst wished to remain at a distance, but I was forever grateful for her support. Even across the divide of "no contact," we were kindred spirits. Mrs. Harpst's final gift firmly cemented this without doubt, that the welfare of animals and fostering the human-animal bond matters.

I turned to Shelly, smiled, and said to her something I was never able to say to our most generous benefactor, "Mrs. Harpst, thank you!"

Ask Dr. Mark:

Should Homeless People Have Pets?

Throughout my career, one of the best parts of my jobs has been getting to talk to people from all walks of life. It's especially rewarding when the other person and I share the same love and value for the human-animal bond.

Doris was one of those people. She was a very helpful and dedicated volunteer at the San Diego Humane Society, of which I was the president and CEO. One day, she knocked on my office door and surprised me with a question, "Dr. Mark, shouldn't we have a law that prohibits homeless people from having an animal?" Before I could respond, she went on to make her case. "I mean, those people can't even take care of themselves. How can we expect them to be able to treat a dog properly?"

In thinking about Doris's question, I knew the rationale behind her asking wasn't to be critical of the homeless. She was coming at this issue from the standpoint of someone who cares deeply about the well-being of dogs. As an upper middle-class woman, I suspected Doris had never been exposed to what it's like to live on the street. Likewise, she couldn't understand what people living without a home might value or what brings purpose to their lives.

My initial surprise at her question quickly turned to appreciation for her concern about animals and also for the opportunity it offered me to show her a different perspective. Years before, when working at the San Francisco SPCA, the team there had given serious thought and real study to this topic, in part, because we had similar concerns.

"Doris," I explained, "in reality when you study the interaction between homeless people and their animals, what you see is nothing less than true love. The majority of hungry street people who have a pet will still share whatever limited resources they have equally with their friend. In fact, sometimes the first few morsels go to the pet before the person."

I went on with a rhetorical question of my own, asking, "How many people who have a home can say they spend even half of their time with their pet?"

Of course, the answer is "not many." I suggested that, in general, the more affluent people are, the less quality time they spend with their pet, not because they don't care, but their lifestyle, the demands of supporting a home, and all the other diversions, simply limit their time.

"Which do you think the dog would want more?" I asked Doris, "24/7 love and companionship with their favorite friend, or to be left alone tied up in a yard or locked in a big house with lots of toys for eight to twelve hours a day?"

It may not be the lap of luxury, but the lap of a homeless person is one that's available 24/7 for their pet. In return, the person without a home gets unconditional love, and on those cold nights on the streets, even shared bodily warmth. In fact, the pet's love for their owner may even be the only true love the person feels they have in their life. It can give them purpose, and with that comes a desire to be there to care for their pet. It can even make the difference for a person to choose sobriety over being in an altered state of mind from drugs or alcohol.

I learned from my parents not to judge people by their looks, and years of practicing veterinary medicine had supported this wise advice. I had often seen the most poorly dressed person do everything possible for their pet, even if they could not easily afford it. On many occasions, I had experienced "street people" using what precious few dollars they had to seek veterinary care for their beloved pets before they would spend it on themselves. Conversely, I have experienced well-dressed individuals with Rolex watches, who could easily afford to top-notch treatment, put their pets at risk because they had a very different value system when it comes to animals.

While the conclusion to Doris' question might at first seem counterintuitive, after my explanation she understood and said, "I see your point, Dr. Mark. Love is love."

Chapter 19

SAMUEL

During my years as president of the SDHS, I had the privilege of handling the acceptance of many estates left to the organization. In a few instances, I even acted as executor. I firmly believed that the individuals who left us their wealth were paying us a great honor. To me, it's one thing to donate to a nonprofit while you're alive and able to see the resulting work done. But it's an incredible act of trust to donate your life's work and resources to an organization when you won't be around to see it used as intended. Because of this, I always tried to understand the essence of what the donor wished their resources be used for and then work together with the SDHS staff to honor that trust.

Samuel was one of those people who had written the SDHS into his will, and Shelly, our director of development, and I had first met him when we were invited, as representatives of the SDHS, to attend a meeting in his attorney's office to discuss his estate plans. Also in attendance at the meeting were Dr. Rose Brown, a veterinarian I knew to be very compassionate and capable, along with two estate attorneys and an individual to record the proceedings. Like many other humane societies, the SDHS was a nonprofit institution that relied on donations for doing its work, so it was routine for Shelly and me to regularly meet with various people interested in supporting our cause of being the community's touchstone for enriching the human-animal bond.

By my estimation, Samuel was a man in his late thirties or early forties. Although he appeared to be in good health and was younger than the typical donor planning for the end of life, Samuel was nevertheless interested in setting up the details of his estate in the event something should happen to him. I was somewhat surprised, then, when Samuel said, "Dr. Goldstein, it's my intention that my estate be left to the San Diego Humane Society. However, I also have my dogs to consider."

As the meeting proceeded, Samuel told us about his beloved dogs, and it became apparent that he wanted to include provisions that any money from his estate would first be used to care for his dogs in totality, both their day-to-day care and any necessary medical care. Beyond this, he wanted the SDHS to handle any arrangements necessary for placing the dogs with a family of Dr. Brown's choosing. Once the costs were covered to care for the dogs as Samuel wished, the remainder of the estate would go to the SDHS.

Shelly and I left the meeting thinking what a caring man Samuel was to think of his dogs as he did in looking out for their welfare. At the same time, we couldn't help wondering if Samuel had some terminal disease that he wasn't disclosing since he gave the distinct impression he felt some urgency to conclude documenting what he wanted.

Three months after our meeting, Shelly came into my office with a shocking announcement. "Samuel has passed away," Shelly told me, having just heard the news herself. I was surprised to hear of his death so soon and with him being such a young age, and thought maybe he, indeed, had a terminal illness.

"That's very sad news," I bemoaned. "We need to inform the staff to make preparations to care for his dogs as he directed."

"There's something else you should know," Shelly continued. "In the paperwork, we not only received a death certificate but an autopsy report." This was curious, since SDHS didn't typically see autopsy reports provided as standard documents in receiving an estate. Shelly said, "Mark, Samuel wasn't physically ill. The report says that Samuel committed suicide."

As the news sunk in, my mind raced with questions of how we could have missed that this compassionate man was so troubled. How had so many people not detected the signs that Samuel's preparations for caring for his pets in the event he was gone indicated his intentions to take his own life? I felt especially confounded because, as a veterinarian, I was conditioned to read nonverbal cues of patients who cannot talk.

I had witnessed other instances of people rescued from the brink of depression by the love of—and for—their animals. But in this case, even when Samuel certainly loved and cared for his dogs, the love he received from them was not enough to keep him from deciding to end his life.

Learning of his suicide was a tragic moment for me, one that has stayed with me to this day. Even in the midst of such heartbreaking misfortune, I looked for a silver lining to the tragedy. I've often been impressed by this deeply affected man, particularly by how a person so lacking in love for himself had so much love for his pets and their future prosperity, that he memorialized what should happen to them after he was no longer there to personally care for them. Ironically, in doing so, Samuel demonstrated that life is precious. Even when he was no longer alive himself, the quality of life for his beloved animals still mattered.

We at the SDHS took this to heart in carrying out Samuel's directives for his estate. We did everything we could to honor him in caring for his beloved dogs in the best ways possible. We found his two furry friends a new home with a loving family, approved by Dr. Brown, and to this day lovingly hold his memory in our hearts.

Chapter 20

MORE THAN ADOPTIONS

Animal welfare organizations around the country—whether nonprofit humane societies and SPCAs or publicly funded shelters—provide services in public safety while working in concert to save the lives of all adoptable homeless animals. While these are often the primary functions that come to mind when people think about what animal welfare groups do, these organizations actually go far beyond that. In recognizing the value and power of the human-animal bond, they engage in many diverse activities to help both people and animals, such as: providing medical services, holding educational classes, running camps for kids, rescuing animals in emergency situations, and many other innovations—all with the goal of strengthening that bond.

One of my favorite examples of this at the San Diego Humane Society was the Listening Ears program. The driving force by Listening Ears was our education manager, Dr. Annie Peterson, an avid animal lover all her life with a special place in her heart for guinea pigs. At SDHS, she was in charge of developing and managing a wide array of curricula to take place either at our campus or at various other locations in the San Diego area. She also coordinated and managed our popular summer camps, attended by as many as 600 children. Annie had a master's degree in counseling psychology and had also worked at the San Diego Zoo for eight years, managing special events and operations. Further, she had earned her doctorate in education, delivering her dissertation on the effect of experience with animals on the reading comprehension skills of students in the seventh grade. She was the perfect candidate for running our education programs.

In working with children and animals, Annie recognized that the presence of a friendly animal breaks down inhibitions in children and helps them come out of their shell. This was especially true when the animal provides positive feedback, such as wagging its tail, cocking an ear, or showing a friendly face in response to whatever the child is doing. When a child is asked to read out loud with a dog in the room, because the animal responds positively no matter how well the child does, the child is encouraged to try and read more.

For a child who has lived through abuse or other ordeals, an animal can feel like their only friend, or someone they can trust in an otherwise unpredictable world. One such child was Ryan. When he was young, Ryan suffered significant trauma, and, in response, he chose not to speak at all.

Through the Listening Ears program put together by Annie, Ryan found love and companionship with a canine friend, and in turn, found his voice. Ryan started in the Pet Pals program, an after-school program at the San Diego Humane Society (SDHS), when he was ten years old. He had been severely traumatized when he was younger and had stopped communicating. He was not able to thrive because of his inhibitions. He was then put in the Listening Ears program at SDHS. Over the course of two years, he interacted with a number of dogs, most often either a pug or a golden retriever. He was left alone with the dogs (still being supervised from a distance) and encouraged to talk to them, and then he progressed to reading to them. Miraculously, he came out of his shell, started to talk, and became much more social.

The dog gave Ryan an audience of unconditional acceptance and was the positive boost that helped him get over a barrier of fear and a lack of self-confidence. The dog not only helped him to speak but to learn how to read! It was a profound experience to witness and offered a compelling lesson in the power of unconditional love and acceptance.

Chapter 21

ANGEL

 **At the opening of the Austen Stowell Animal** Care Center, new home to the San Diego Humane Society, I heard various people in the crowd ask, "Who is Austen Stowell?" as they speculated about the namesake for the new facility. The new center was a landmark achievement, and the finishing touch to the San Diego Campus for Animal Care, itself a reflection of a groundbreaking partnership between public and private animal welfare entities.

Public agencies for animals have a long history rooted in providing for the needs of a community. During medieval times in Europe, a villager's free-roaming livestock might be taken to a communal holding pen called the "pound," where owners could reclaim their animals by paying a fee to the poundmaster. Over time, the scope of pounds expanded as industrialization grew and populations shifted from villages and towns to expanding cities. Here, public services also sought to control animals that posed public nuisances or health hazards, such as the spread of disease, due to their overpopulation in urban areas.

The rise of private animal welfare organizations began in the 1800s with the creation of humane societies, such as the Society for the Prevention of Cruelty to Animals (SPCA). The first SPCAs

179

were primarily concerned with the plight of abused workhorses, but quickly broadened their battles to other acts of cruelty such as rat, dog, and cock fighting. The United States' first formal adoption program for companion animals was established in Philadelphia in 1869 by the Women's Humane Society, where the term "shelter" was first introduced into the lexicon of animal care.

A century later, thousands of disparate public and private entities across the country provided some form of animal services via any mix of organizations. Governmental agencies were primarily tasked with public safety responsibilities, such as animal control, and nonprofits like the humane society or SPCA, would provide shelter and adoption services. Depending on the municipality, towns would have either one or both of these types of services. In towns without a public agency, often a private nonprofit would be contracted to provide public services.

Despite agendas that often overlapped, these organizations frequently remained at odds and could even be combative with one another. The reasons for this vary, but often at the center of the conflict were well-intentioned, passionate individuals who wanted to help animals but had insufficient resources, leaving them feeling alienated. This frustration was easily misdirected into disrespecting another organization, which then escalated into public verbal arguments.

Part of why I felt so proud to be part of the San Diego animal welfare community was the incredible accomplishment of the county, city, and SDHS in successfully overcoming any animosity and replacing it with open communication, mutual respect, and a desire to publicly recognize each other's accomplishments. By becoming partners, all organizations were encouraged to share the challenges they faced and together find solutions.

The results were a newfound alignment and shared mission to

collectively create a safety net for animals in San Diego, including the joint development of the nation's first collocated facilities for public and private animal welfare organizations. The San Diego Campus for Animal Care was designed to house the county's Department of Animal Services and SDHS. The grand opening in 2003 of SDHS's new Austen Stowell Animal Care Center was a celebration that marked the completion of construction and the fruition of years of planning and hard work.

"Dr. Mark," a man asked, "Can you tell me who Austen Stowell is?"

"Of course," I half chuckled, "Austen Stowell is the figment of an angel's imagination." He looked at me quizzically as I continued, "Actually, it's a fictitious name," Austen Stowell was the name chosen by an anonymous donor we refer to as our 'Angel.'"

I first heard of this Angel two years before. Soon after starting my job as the CEO and president of SDHS in 2001, the topic "Angel" was on the agenda for one of my many meetings with Shelly Stuart, our senior vice president of development. "Dr. Mark," Shelly said, "we need to talk about the grant application for Akaloa." I hadn't heard of Akaloa so asked her to explain. "Akaloa means 'wind through the pines,' and is the name given to the charitable foundation of our Angel. The foundation has been supporting us for some time now. Each year we go through an application process, but the foundation has consistently been contributing over $100,000 annually."

I heard the dollar amount and was thrilled to hear of the foundation's support, but something else was on my mind, so I asked, "What do you mean it's the foundation of our Angel?" What Angel?"

"A few years ago a woman named Cathy Hopper came to SDHS to meet with our past president. She said she represented a donor who was interested in supporting the work here but only on the condition of remaining anonymous. Cathy was explicit that even an attempt to identify the donor would jeopardize any future funding, not only for SDHS but other Akaloa beneficiaries."

When I asked if we knew anything at all about the Angel, she replied, "Not really. We don't even know if it's a 'them' or an individual. We were simply asked to consider referring to this donor as our Angel. Beyond that, we only know it's our Angel's intention to make a difference in the world, and so far, SDHS has been judged worthy of Akaloa's grant-making."

"Well, hopefully, that continues to be the case," I smiled. "We can surely use the help!" At the time, the construction slated for 80,000 square feet of new facilities came with a price tag of $21 million. The county's portion was $11 million, which they quickly met with an outpouring of public support and $2 million in generous grants from two philanthropists. As a nonprofit, SDHS would need to cover its $10 million share with charitable donations. The county was off and running to build their 36,000 square feet of the campus, but we still had a lot of fundraising to do. Shelly and I went to work completing Akaloa's grant application. We had little clue for how our Angel might judge our plans, but we laid them out as clearly as possible.

By the spring of 2003, our Angel had contributed over $2 million to the fundraising effort. Over the two years since Shelly first informed me of our incognito supporter, we learned from Cathy that the mystery Angel who established Akaloa was a singular woman. The foundation was set up to support a limited number of named beneficiaries, one of which was SDHS, all sponsored under the same terms of anonymity.

One day Shelly came to my office with an exciting proposition. "Dr. Mark, I just received a call from Cathy. She wants to know if it'd be possible for our Angel to come after hours to meet us and tour the construction site." We were both dumbfounded and ecstatic. We knew from previous conversations with Cathy that our Angel had never met with any of Akaloa's grantees, so meeting her would not only be a privilege but also meant we were being trusted to respect her wishes and privacy.

"Yes, of course," I said. "What a priceless honor. Please let her know she can come anytime it's convenient for her." Shelly then set an appointment, reassured Cathy that we would ensure our Angel's anonymity, and kept the news to ourselves while we prepared for her impending visit. We felt like kids anxious for the arrival of a secret gift.

At the appointed hour on the day of this highly anticipated visit, Shelly and I made our way to the front of the construction site to greet the arriving party. After a few false alarms, cars driving by without stopping, a van pulled up and slowed to park. "Do you think that could be her?" Shelly said. "I was expecting a luxurious car, maybe even a limo with a chauffeur since a few people are coming. I mean no offense, but that van looks like it's seen better days!"

The vehicle parked, the doors opened, and out from the driver's side jumped a spry, older woman. She was modestly dressed with no outward signs of wealth. In truth, someone might have thought she couldn't afford the ramshackle van, but this woman had a smile that could make you laugh from twenty feet away. I knew immediately, she was our Angel. As the others were getting out of the vehicle, the grinning driver walked straight up to me, gave me a big hug, thanked me for the work the SDHS staff and I were doing, and then enthusiastically declared, "Let's go see this place!"

Along for the ride were Cathy Hopper, who introduced us to two others, Cheryl Wilson and Christy Morse, saying they were friends of our Angel. With everyone present and accounted for, we started the tour at the front of the property, where I pointed out the building on the left, recently finished and operational for the County. On the right, the exterior of the SDHS structure was complete, and in between the buildings, the hardscape elements of two courtyards had recently been constructed.

"I can see it's really starting to come together now," Cathy said.

"Yes, we're excited about the progress," I agreed. "Work is now starting on the building's interior and other finishing touches. Soon we'll have trees and shrubs and flowers planted in the landscape, and the inner courtyard will have sculptures and a fountain." I led them through the entryway to the inside of the SDHS building. "This will be 44,000 square feet of space dedicated to supporting all aspects of the human-animal bond," I said.

"It's very spacious," our Angel chimed in, "much better than the older building."

I guided the group through the cavernous atrium and turned down hallways on the left and right. "Yes, we'll have a lot more room, but that doesn't mean more corridors lined with cages. Instead, we'll have cozy 'living rooms' for dogs and cats," I explained as we strolled along. "Our campus will provide an entirely different experience for everyone, including the animals."

"Dr. Mark, I've noticed you're referring to this as a 'campus,'" said Christy Morse, "but I've never heard that word used for a shelter before."

My mind thought back to the decision to name the property. During a meeting between the stakeholders at the county, city, and SDHS, we debated the options. The most poignant moment for me was when someone said, "I'm having a problem understanding the term 'campus.' It makes it sound like there's education going on there." I suppressed the desire to say, "Well, yes, duh!" but instead calmly explained that SDHS will provide many opportunities for people to learn at the facilities. The idea of "education" at an animal shelter was clearly new territory for some people, but in the end, the group voted and chose to call our developing joint venture the San Diego Campus for Animal Care.

"You're right about that, Christy. In fact, we're the first animal welfare facility in the country to use the term 'campus.' Our vision is to incorporate a variety of programs that engage and educate, so the term 'campus' helps to bring attention to these services. Further, we see the campus itself acting as a community center, a foundation of learning, sharing, and caring, where people will come to be involved in animal welfare in new ways. It's not just about getting people in the door to take home a new pet. We believe the more people know about caring for animals and the mutual benefit of the human-animal bond, the better off the whole community will be, both for animals and people.

"For instance, when a family does take home a new pet, we want that adoption to be the beginning of a long-term relationship. We don't expect 100 percent of adoptions to be lifelong because a myriad of circumstances can happen in a home and compel people to relinquish a pet. From landlords not allowing pets, to a change in finances, divorce, military deployments, and many more things beyond someone's control can force them to give up a furry friend even though it breaks their heart. For such cases, SDHS provides an important function by giving those animals shelter and working to find them a new home. In other instances, education for pet families can help to avoid them giving up a pet by arming them with information on how to handle common problems. For instance, a primary reason cats are brought in to shelters is inappropriate elimination in the house—in other words, they 'go' outside the litter box. When people adopt a cat, we can inform them of what to look for and how to handle this if it happens. The more knowledge a family has for success, in this case curbing unwanted behavior, the better chance they'll have for keeping their new pet and with a better experience for everyone in the home."

"That makes sense to me," Christy commented. "Can you tell us more about your programs?"

"Sure. I already talked about education for new pet owners. Another example of adult and youth programs we will provide are positive reinforcement behavior training classes for pet owners. The course will give owners tools for interacting with their pet in a productive manner and also teach them and their animals good behaviors. In constructing the new campus, we're developing a space where people can gather to learn, socialize, have fun, and bring their pets. Another component of our plans is to continue and grow our outreach programs to let people know what we have to offer and invite them to join us."

"I'm glad to hear that, Dr. Mark," our Angel said. "The telethon on TV is what prompted my first donation to the humane society. It deeply touched me, so I sent a check for $100,000 because I love my little dogs and want others to experience that same joy."

This warmed the cockles of my veterinary heart. Our annual telethons were well-received by viewers and helped immeasurably to raise awareness and funding and boost adoptions, but it was nice to know this was how our Angel found us. With our $10 million fundraising campaign underway, the telethons were more crucial than ever as we relied on donations ranging from $1 to thousands. We had collected over $8 million to date, but with so far to go to reach $10 million, we were counting on the upcoming telethon to help us inch closer to the finish line.

"Thank you—both for the generous support, and for being the perfect example of what we hope our outreach programs can accomplish," I replied to our Angel. "In addition to traditional outreach, we're involved in the community in many ways, such as pet-assisted therapy, investigating animal cruelty and neglect, rescuing animals in emergency situations, as well as running fun events like our Dog Walk to raise money. Of course, the size and scope of the new campus will also expand our capacity to help more animals and provide them better care."

Although the space was bare, I took our guests into the back area of the building "Here's the location of our new animal hospital. We're going from a 500-square-foot treatment room in the old building to a 2,300-square-foot medical center. We'll be able to provide comprehensive veterinary care; everything from spaying and neutering to life-saving surgeries and therapies for animals with chronic disease. Just because an animal is homeless doesn't mean it should get inadequate healthcare while waiting to be adopted. We never want to take the life of an animal just because the resources and skill aren't available."

"Although the space is empty, it's impressive to know this will more than quadruple the current medical facilities," Christy said.

"Yes, we're looking forward to having those capabilities available as soon as possible. SDHS has already achieved the goal of never euthanizing a healthy or treatable animal, but part of our role in working with the County Department of Animal Services is to help achieve this same goal countywide in their various shelters. The veterinary hospital will be a key element in getting there. Not only will the size of the area be bigger, but also the scope of services it affords us to provide will increase exponentially as well. Also, we've figured out a way to make use of the veterinary center for our educational programs as well."

"How will you do that?" our Angel asked.

I walked a few feet away and pointed to where large electro-static windows would be installed in the future. "When children and adults alike tour the hospital or are participating in a program, they'll be able to look through windows and observe the medical staff at work. More than that, the windows will be electrostatic. If something is going on that would be uncomfortable for some-one to watch, the staff can push a button, and the windows will become opaque."

I turned back to the group and saw our Angel welling with emotions. "I am so proud to be part of this," she said through tears of joy. "You have thought of everything."

I still didn't know her name, but in seeing our Angel so visibly moved, all at once it seemed I saw her essence, and in that magi-cal moment I felt profoundly connected to this woman of deep caring and compassion. "I'm glad to know you're pleased with what we're doing. We know this wouldn't be possible without your help, so we're grateful you're part of this as well—and very happy you came here today to see the campus for yourself."

"It's been my pleasure, Dr. Mark," our Angel said. "However, it's getting late, so it's time for us to go." I thanked them for their visit as Shelly and I escorted the group back to the parking lot, where we said our goodbyes.

The next morning, I got a phone call from Christy saying our Angel wanted to talk to me, so we set a time. When we spoke later in the day, after a few brief pleasantries she quickly got to the point. "Dr. Mark, how much will it cost to complete that silly campaign for the campus?"

The SDHS team was working hard to raise the balance of the $10 million, but our board estimated it would take another twelve to eighteen months to finish the campaign. I told her we'd need

$1.57 million. With great pleasure and resolution, she announced, "You will have your check next week!"

I was stunned. Her astonishing statement startled me so much that I almost couldn't breathe. With this additional donation, our Angel's contribution to the building campaign totaled over $4 million—and I still didn't know her name. "This is unbelievable!" I exuded, emotionally overcome. "This means we'll be able to finish the building now without taking on debt. Thank you! From the bottom of my heart, thank you!"

Months later, at the grand opening of the Austen Stowell Animal Care Center, her name was still a mystery to me. But by then, her smiling face was a familiar sight from the many late-night visits she had made to see the continuing construction of the new campus.

"Who's Austen Stowell?" I heard the question again. As I explained to another person at the event about the origins of the "fictitious" Austen Stowell, nearby I spied Cathy Hopper delightfully giggling with unbounded glee. Over the coming years, this was the pattern. Our Angel, or her representative, would attend the events of her charitable beneficiaries and merrily laugh with eyes twinkling while others hypothesized about the identity of the donor.

Despite this ongoing mystery, our Angel's contributions were the financial jumpstarts that catalyzed a tsunami of support that poured in from many others and made it possible for us to make our dreams turn into reality. Within a few years, SDHS went from a modest, traditional shelter on Sherman Street with a staff of 60 people to over 260 staff members and 2,000 volunteers on four campuses. Together, we developed and maintained nationally recognized programs for education, rehoming pets, and other innovations, such as the nation's first orphan kitten nursery, to extend a safety net to animals. Further, the Austen Stowell Animal Care Center became the heart of animal welfare in San Diego, with popular programs like our summer camp for kids, which infused opportunities for over 600 campers to learn how to humanely care for and interact with animals while enjoying fun activities that summer camps typically afford a child.

The campuses also revolutionized the nature of what was possible. Once thought to be unreachable and almost unimaginable, the goal of helping all adoptable, healthy and treatable animals in the San Diego region was achieved and continues to the present day.

This kind of undertaking and success would not have been possible without the hard, selfless work of the staff and volunteers, along with the confidence and financial support of a caring community, and notably, the backing of our Angel. Once the building was complete, our Angel often came to the shelter in the evenings to visit the animals, where she sparkled with childlike exhilaration at what we had created together at SDHS.

Three years after the grand opening of the Austen Stowell Animal Care Center, SDHS held another ceremony, one to rename the building. In attendance were members of the original tour group, but the sunshiny smile of our Angel was missing.

"Dr. Mark, who is Austen Stowell?" someone asked me the familiar question. This time I knew the correct answer. The name was not fictitious after all. "Austen Stowell was the father of our Angel. Austen and Stowell were his first and middle names. The event today is to change the name of the building to include their family name, and to honor our Angel, who recently passed away."

When I heard the news of our Angel's death, I was deeply saddened to know I'd never see her again, or—under the sign with the building's new name—hear laughter when someone wondered about her identity as they asked: "Who is Austen Stowell?" But as I pulled on the cloth to unveil the new name of the building, I felt she must be smiling on us, as angels are said to do. "Ladies and gentlemen," I announced, "It gives me great pleasure to rededicate the home of the San Diego Humane Society and SPCA as the Austen S. Cargill Animal Care Center."

Until after her death in 2006, I didn't know that our Angel was an heiress to the vast Cargill family fortune. It was her grandfather, William Wallace Cargill, who, in 1865, founded what would become the largest private company in the United States, Cargill Inc., a global agribusiness producing commodities from grains to livestock, still owned and operated by his descendants to this day.

Born in 1920, Margaret Cargill was raised in Minneapolis. As a member of the prominent Cargill family, she had a traditional debutante "coming out" party and was often mentioned in newspaper society columns during her youth. However, she had no aspirations to enter the stratosphere of high society. Instead, she spent time with friends, traveled, and explored her interest in the arts, which she studied at the University of Minnesota and where she received a degree in art education. Throughout her life, she enjoyed weaving and textiles and cultivated her skills and knowledge of folk art.

After Margaret's father resigned as chairman of the board at Cargill in 1953, her parents moved to Pasadena, California. A few years later, she moved from Minnesota to be near them and quickly acclimated to her new home. She liked living in California, in part, because people didn't instantly recognize her family name. She could feel free to go anywhere as herself, and not be encumbered by her money or family's social status. This value was so vital to the fabric of her being that in her philanthropy she went to extremes to remain anonymous.

In 1957, Margaret was devastated when her father suddenly passed away while on a fishing trip. It prompted her first tribute to him a few years later when she sponsored and christened the nation's most powerful towboat operating in inland waterways as the *Austen S. Cargill.*

Our Angel didn't care about leading a lavish lifestyle. What mattered to her was making a positive difference in the world. If she saw things that weren't right, she wanted to right them. She desired to keep the focus on the work. Her declaration to cover the remaining $1.57 million of the SDHS building campaign was the perfect example of this, and one of the most startling moments of my career. I cannot overemphasize how much of an impact this angelic woman had on my life with her generosity and her philosophy for how she lived her life.

While Margaret was alive, I didn't know her name, but still, I knew the character of our Angel. In my thirty years working in animal welfare, I never met a more humble, compassionate person of such immense wealth who cared about people and animals—and cared nothing about being recognized for it.

Although a billionaire, incredibly, she eschewed the trappings of wealth and found her greatest joy in giving. Her inheritance afforded her the opportunity to make a difference for others in ways most can only imagine. She was changing the world—and she loved it.

Our Angel spent the last years of her life surrounded by friends like Christy, Cathy, Paul Busch, and Naomi Horsager, who aided her in identifying how her wealth would continue to help the world be a better place in perpetuity. Under their expertise and care, Margaret A. Cargill Philanthropies (MACP) was created to encompass oversight for Margaret's multiple charitable foundations, including the Margaret A. Cargill Foundation, the Anne

Ray Foundation named for her mother, and Akaloa, all of which totaled $4 billion in assets after the settlement of Margaret's estate.

Margaret's main philanthropic interests were making a difference in animal welfare, disaster relief, women and children, the environment, and the arts. At SDHS, we were fortunate to have her support. At the time of her death, our Angel had donated over $10 million and helped to create extraordinary synergy for the human-animal bond and its value in the community.

In the years since her passing, I've had the opportunity to see dozens of photographs taken of Margaret throughout her life. What's striking is to behold her bright smile radiating in every shot. She was as happy a person as I've ever met, funny, loving, warm, and generous. Because of her need for privacy, I felt blessed to have her trust in visiting SDHS so often. She was a shining example for me and others. I only wish more people could have known her.

If it's true that wealth merely amplifies a person's character, Margaret Cargill was the personification of joy, selfless giving, and a *genuine* angel.

Chapter 22

KATRINA

When natural disasters strike, people some- times lose their homes and are often separated from their beloved pets, who either perish or become lost in the aftermath. Animal welfare organizations often band together far from the affected region. Such was the case in the aftermath of Hurricane Katrina, the catastrophic Category 5 hurricane that raked through the Caribbean and Florida before it laid waste to Louisiana and Mississippi on August 29, 2005. Although it did not take a direct hit, greater New Orleans was devastated when its levee system failed after the actual storm had passed, submerging large parts of the city under water, killing many people and animals, and destroying homes and businesses.

Days after the catastrophic storm hit the greater New Orleans area, SDHS deployed staff members and first responders to work side by side with the devastated and overwhelmed Louisiana SPCA. With the animal welfare facilities in New Orleans destroyed by flooding, a makeshift shelter was created sixty miles west near Baton Rouge at the Lamar-Dixon Expo Center. In the weeks and months that followed, a cavalry of rescue groups mobilized at 5:30 AM every day to the New Orleans area and returned to the Lamar-Dixon Expo Center after dark with traumatized animals of all kinds, from dogs and cats to horses, pigs, and snakes. Ultimately, it's estimated that over 15,000 animals were rescued.

The sheer number of animals necessitated that shelters and fostering agencies from across the country step in to help since Louisiana had no facility large enough to accommodate them. T. Boone Pickens and the employees of his company, BP Capital, donated $7 million to the relief effort, which provided funding for airplanes to help evacuate the myriad of pets ripped apart from their families.

From the masses of lost animals, 102 dogs were flown to San Diego to escape the carnage and be cared for by a coalition of animal welfare organizations lead by SDHS. Since 1970, when SDHS established the first Animal Rescue Reserve of specially trained staff and volunteers able to assist any animal in an emergency, the organization was relied upon to assist anywhere needed on the frontline of disasters.

With the pooches 1,800 miles from home and safe in SDHS facilities and other local animal shelters, the daunting task of finding their families fell to Senior Vice President of Animal Care Renee Harris and her team. Renee was the poster child animal lover. She had volunteered and worked in animal welfare organizations since she was just twelve years old.

Renee was elated when she was able to connect one Katrina survivor, Marian, with her dog Vickie, a sweet mixed breed terrier. After pouring through reams of information collected by the first responders and conducting relentless investigative work, including countless phone calls to explore and confirm solid facts about a family and their pet's identity, Renee had found a match in Marian and her dog. On the phone, Renee said, "Marian, thank you for sending over the pictures. We definitely have your dog here in San Diego!"

"I can't believe it," responded Marian when she spoke to Renee on the phone. "Oh my goodness, it's a miracle!"

Renee said, "We'd like to invite you to come to San Diego to reunite with Vickie and take her home." She continued, "Your dog's been through a lot of trauma, so we're not comfortable just loading her on a plane without first reacquainting her with a loved one."

"What do you mean?" Marian questioned. "I'm sorry, but my home is gone and I've just lost everything. I can't afford to come to San Diego."

"I know, Marian," Renee said. After so many phone conversations between them, Renee knew Marian lived in the Ninth Ward neighborhood of New Orleans, an area stricken by great poverty and ruthlessly devastated by the hurricane. "After everything you've been through, we feel it's the least we can do to pay for you to come out to San Diego and be rejoined with your dog before taking her home."

"I don't know," she hesitated." Throughout the reunification process after Hurricane Katrina, we were surprised to find that people were nearly always skeptical at the offer to travel to San Diego on SDHS's dime. The initial shock of disbelief was quickly followed by an assumption that some sort of strings would be attached, so they often felt uncertain about what to do. Fortunately, Renee had a gift for quickly discerning and easily handling a person's concerns.

In one case, for instance, SDHS flew a father and son out from Louisiana to rejoin them with their dog, Tiger. While the pair was in their hotel room in the evening, Renee received a phone call from the father who politely wanted to clarify whether they could order food from the hotel restaurant and have the costs covered. Earlier in the day, Renee learned that the family had never stayed in a hotel and came from great poverty, so she quickly confirmed that SDHS would pay for their meal. However, after he expressed further reluctance about going to the restaurant, then about ordering from the room service menu, suddenly Renee had an epiphany: the man couldn't read, nor could his son.

Not wanting to embarrass them by bringing attention to that supposition, she instead said, "You know what, let's make this easy. When we hang up just dial 'zero' on the phone and ask for room service. When they answer, tell them you want to order a steak, or whatever you like, and it will be delivered to your room." The grateful man ended the phone call with an exuberant thanks to Renee, and to the SDHS, for everything they done to reunite his family with their beloved Tiger.

Sensing Marian's apprehension, Renee reassured, "Marian, I don't want you to worry about a thing. There will be nothing more for you to do than relax in San Diego for a few days and get to know your dog again. SDHS will cover all the expenses and make sure you both return home together."

"This is unbelievable," Marian burst into merry rejoicing as she wrapped her head around the idea. "It's another miracle! Renee, you're an angel!"

A short time later, Renee was at the San Diego International Airport, happily holding up a sign with Marian's name on it so Marian could find her. Although they'd never met in person, the two had gotten along famously on the phone, and Renee was looking forward to meeting her.

I had expected to hear reports of a happy first meeting when she came back to the office, but instead Renee returned confused and unsettled. "When she came up and introduced herself as Marian, naturally I gave her a hug," Renee related. "She accepted the hug, but I sensed she must have felt tentative or even trepidatious, but I can't imagine why. I don't get it, Dr. Mark," Renee said. "She seemed so different on the phone. I felt like we were friends, but when I picked her up at the airport she barely said a word to me all the way here."

"Maybe she's tired from the trip," I speculated. "Perhaps she'll feel better once she sees Vickie again."

For an animal that's been through extreme traumas, reuniting them with their family isn't necessarily as easy as it might sound. The rescued dogs of Hurricane Katrina had been stripped from their loved ones, homes, and favorite chair, to survive winds lifting them off their feet, swimming for their life, or worse conditions, then being taken by a stranger to cavernous facilities with hundreds of other animals being placed on an airplane for the first time in their lives (something with which they would be totally unfamiliar) before eventually shipping off to San Diego to a world they didn't know.

Although Renee had explained the reality of the situation, I knew I needed to reinforce this in the likely event that the reunification would not meet Marian's expectations. I said, "Marian, we have Vickie waiting in the other room, but before we bring the two of you together, it's important you're prepared to see her again."

"I don't understand. What do you mean?" she asked.

I said, "With everything Vickie's been through, we don't know how she'll react to seeing you. It's not uncommon for a dog who's endured as much as she has to not immediately recognize a familiar face. If that happens, I don't want you to be surprised."

"Dr. Mark, I can't imagine that. I've had her since she was a puppy. It would break my heart if she didn't know who I was," Marian said.

"We understand," Renee comforted, "but if she doesn't seem to recognize you, it will be best to keep your distance and give her some space. Running up with hugs and kisses may not be welcome from her point of view."

Having prepped Marian for the possibilities, we brought Vickie into the room. "Come here, girl," Marian gently coaxed. The little dog looked up at her and seemed curious but timidly backed away. Over and over, the minutes slowly ticked by with the two friends remaining apart. Marian withheld her natural inclination to throw her arms around her best friend, while the ragamuffin dog looked Marion up and down from her outpost on the floor, not quite sure what to make of her. As the moments dragged on, tears started to well in Marian's eyes as she struggled to contain an emotional deluge. Much like the levees in her hometown, Marian's will had been stretched to the limit.

"My poor little buddy," Marian contemplated, "What you must've been going through." As much as it may have hurt Marian not to be recognized, it was the realization of how much her furry friend had suffered that pained her the most as she worked to keep her emotions in check.

"Oh, I nearly forgot," she softly said as she reached into her purse. Out of the handbag came a raggedy chew toy, one that had seen better days but was kept likely because it was so loved. She gave it a good squeeze and it sounded a faint squeak.

Vickie's ears perked up at the noise but otherwise she remained motionless in her position on the floor. Marian gripped the toy and squeezed again repeatedly. In a flash, as though the sound of a foghorn had instantly dissipated a misty blanket of amnesia, suddenly the little dog was up and running, cheerfully barking into Marian's arms.

"Oh, Vickie, it's good to see you, too!" Marian reveled as tears of joy overwhelmed the emotional dam and streamed down her face. "It's good to have you back. Now everything will be all right."

In the coming days, Marian recharged her batteries with some much-needed relaxation at her hotel, and warmed up to the SDHS staff—especially to Renee—as she spent time with Vickie at the shelter. Marian blossomed into the woman Renee had gotten to know on the phone, warm and bighearted.

The time came for Marian and Vickie to fly home to Louisiana, so Renee gave them a ride to the airport. "Marian, I hope you don't mind me asking, but I've been wondering something. After all our talking on the phone before you came to San Diego, when you first arrived I thought you seemed tentative and withdrawn. I was wondering what that was about?"

"Dear," Marian explained, "when I got off the plane and you saw I was black, I assumed you wouldn't care about me or my dog!"

Renee now recognized the reasons for the unusual initial reception when she greeted Marian at the airport. It never occurred to Renee that the color of Marian's skin would have been the cause of her initial distance, or even possibly her hesitation to come in the first place. However, in Marian's world, she often experienced both cultural and economic segregation, so she had braced herself for the worst in coming to San Diego to reunite with her four-legged friend.

When they reached the airport, Renee bid Marian a fond farewell. "Well, I guess this is goodbye. Thank you for coming out, Marian; it's been so good to finally meet you and see you back together with Vickie."

"No, Renee, thank you. Having Vickie back, it's like getting my hope back. I'm so grateful to you and everyone who's made this possible. Thank you, thank you so much!" And with that, Marian put her arms around Renee and almost squeezed the life out of her as she said repeatedly said "thank you" while tears flowed freely down her cheeks.

Upon returning to the campus, Renee was giddy about having broken the ice with her friend and filled me in on what Marian had shared. I felt awful that Marian's life experiences had convinced her everyone would relate to her as "black" and not respect her as a human being, irrespective of color. SDHS was in the business of saving animals and helping people from all walks of life. We were not naive to how cruel the world could be, but when it's in your face, it shakes you to your core. We felt blessed that we had the opportunity to show Marian another side of humanity and bring unconditional love into her life with the return of her dog, Vickie.

All told, Renee and her team created joyful reunions for forty-four dogs and their families. Of the thousands of animals torn from their homes during Hurricane Katrina ultimately less than 20 percent rejoined their families, so although we hadn't been able to locate every owner, we were grateful for what we had accomplished.

It was an unexpected gift to witness the goodness of each owner. SDHS flew them out and put them up in a nice hotel, where they effectively had a blank check to cover expenses. In every case, without exception, everyone showed gratitude and never took advantage of our hospitality. Further, like Marian, all went home not only with their dog but renewed optimism about the future.

From such experiences, I became very mindful of the opportunities afforded me by the nurturing world I had been blessed to grow up in. Also, to understand why well-funded, successful animal welfare organizations are part of the fabric that supports a healthy community. Most deeply, it reinforced in me how important unconditional love is from our pets, as is unconditional help of strangers to people in the face of great adversity.

Chapter 23

WALLIS

 **"Donations are the lifeblood of a nonprofit** organization, so we were excited when The Annenberg Foundation phoned with a request for Ms. Wallis Annenberg to tour the San Diego Humane Society campus. The reputation of the foundation was well known to the SDHS team, so we considered it an honor that she wanted to see our work and set a date for the visit.

The Annenberg Foundation was established in 1989 by Ms. Annenberg's father, Walter Annenberg, once American ambassador to the United Kingdom, and publishing magnate who presided over a vast communications empire of newspapers, radio and television stations, and national magazines such as *TV Guide* and *Seventeen*. Upon selling his business interests, the Annenbergs dedicated themselves to philanthropic endeavors and set up the foundation with $1.2 billion.

In prepping for Ms. Annenberg's visit, SDHS staff took extra care to ensure the grounds and facilities looked their best. Proud of the campus design, we were eager to show it off and share our learnings with an organization that had extraordinary means to extend the reach of advancing animal welfare in other regions.

As a nonprofit institution continually tasked with raising funds, the team hoped SDHS might benefit in the future with support from the Annenberg Foundation. However, without question, we understood that a request for backing while Ms. Annenberg was at SDHS would be off the table as it would be unprofessional and "bad form," given the nature of the meeting. The standard protocol to apply for a grant or other benefaction was to research and follow the defined processes set up by the charitable organization.

I went to the airport to greet our visitor and escort her to our facility. With my hand extended, I said, "Ms. Annenberg, welcome to San Diego."

"Thank you," she replied, "but please call me Wallis. I insist." I immediately felt an affinity for Wallis as her warm demeanor put me at ease. I was impressed that she was willing to invest the time and energy to see our work for herself. "Dr. Mark," she said, "I'd like you to meet Leonard Aube, our executive director." I shook Leonard's hand, then greeted Wallis's beloved pets, two Westies who I learned traveled with her everywhere. The dogs were excited, and joyously greeted me like an old friend. Look how much the dogs like Dr. Mark!" she bubbled. "Aren't they cute?"

With everyone present and accounted for, we made our way to my SUV where the dogs happily jumped in for a ride, and we took off. "We've heard good things about the success of the humane society in San Diego," Leonard said. "We're looking forward to seeing it in person and getting some ideas for Wallis's dream of creating a similar campus in Los Angeles County."

"Thank you, Leonard. I appreciate that," I replied as we drove along. "I'm very proud of what our team is accomplishing, so it means a lot to have you and Wallis take the time to come down and see what we're doing."

"We appreciate you having us, Dr. Mark," Wallis offered. "This is my passion project. There is nothing that gives me more joy than my dogs. I consider them my family. I believe our companion animals bring such value to our lives that I want to create a space that can foster the human-animal bond in new ways in Los Angeles."

The three of us chatted about our love of animals and their importance to the community until we reached Gaines Street in Linda Vista at the western end of Mission Valley. Driving onto the campus, I noted that the land was adjacent to the land of the old county shelter. "Part of what makes our campus so unique is it's a state-of-the-art facility shared between SDHS and the County of San Diego," I explained. "It is the first animal shelter in the nation designed for joint use between public and private entities."

In 1999, in response to public outcry about the dilapidated condition of municipal animal shelters in the region, the City and County of San Diego joined forces to address the issue. In exemplary fashion, differences were put aside to approve the construction of a new campus and to collaborate with SDHS in doing so. In 2003, $21 million later, the San Diego Campus for Animal Care opened to the public.

I turned left into the parking lot where the party of five and I exited the vehicle and walked to the front of the campus with its expansive courtyard brightened by flowers and swaying palm trees.

"Would anyone care for a 'yappacino?' Or perhaps a 'hot chocolate lab?'" I offered as we came to the sidewalk cafe managed by SDHS, a space designed to welcome visitors to relax and enjoy barista-style coffees and gourmet snacks in comfortable surroundings.

"No, thank you," came the replies, "but what a great idea."

"Yes, the cafe is more than a spot to grab a drink or get a bite to eat," I explained. "A couple might stop to celebrate their adoption of a new family member, or someone can find comfort and a listening ear after coming to say goodbye to a suffering animal. Also, dogs can practice good behavior and socialize with others in a safe place that serves food." The cafe was a common area meant to reflect and foster the value given to the animals that enrich our lives. Moving past the cafe, on the left was the Kroc-Copley Animal Shelter, named for Joan Kroc, widow of Ray Kroc, known as the founder of McDonald's, and Helen Copley, former publisher of the *San Diego Union-Tribune*, who each contributed $2 million to the shelter's construction. On the right was the building that housed SDHS.

At the far end of the front courtyard, the two structures were connected by a common, walled walkway across the front of which read the shared goal of the organizations: "Dedicated to Saving the Life of Every Adoptable Animal."

Five beautiful archways traversed the length of the wall. We walked through the center arch and entered another courtyard. Lining the second courtyard perimeter was a series of walled walkways with similar arches, all of which created a rectangular inner sanctum with lush foliage surrounding a water feature of bronzed cats and dogs at play. On the walls were inspiring quotes speaking to the wondrous nature of the human-animal bond.

"Dr. Mark, this is absolutely beautiful!" Wallis exclaimed. "I love the layout of the buildings and the feel of the space."

"Yes, we're very proud," I said. "There's been a lot of attention to detail given to making this a friendly and pleasant environment. We even had a *feng shui* expert help on a pro bono basis to create a harmonious setting by incorporating the Chinese practice of placing buildings and furniture according to how they'll affect the flow of positive and negative energy. Here, I'll show you more of what I mean inside." We walked through the entry doors into the SDHS atrium, an open space with skylights curving across the length of the vast room filling it with natural sunlight from above as music played softly in the background.

"It's so peaceful and inviting," Leonard said. "Nothing like the dreary shelters I've seen."

I couldn't have agreed more. "This facility is meant to be more than a physical space for housing animals; it's the cornerstone of a more progressive way of thinking. Today, most shelters aren't places people want to be. They walk in to the sound of barking and meowing and the smell of bad odors. But gloom-and-doom doesn't work. We want people to walk onto our campus and experience a peaceful and enjoyable atmosphere.

"During my years managing zoos in Boston and Los Angeles, I learned that changing the environment of the animals from concrete and bars to a habitat that resembles a natural environment transforms the experience for visitors as well, from people gawking at animals and feeling sorry for them into a lifelong memory of learning filled with adventure and education. At SDHS, we want our campus to do the same thing for the animals we love as our pets." After making introductions to some of the SDHS staff at the reception center, we headed down a spacious hallway to the left.

"Leonard," Wallis said, "Come over here. You have to see this." Wallis was standing in front of a window peering into a twelve-by-twelve-foot room. "See? It looks like a little apartment," she declared. "All of the rooms do."

As we moved down the hallway of windows on both sides, each room featured a different type of décor, transforming the space into a temporary "home" for an adoptable animal. Each space was a place where someone's future pet would not only be comfortable and less stressed than in a typical shelter setting but could learn that rugs aren't meant for peeing and furniture legs are not chew toys.

"Dr. Mark," Leonard said, "this is incredible. How did you do this?"

"The credit goes to an army of talented people," I said. "For example, each of these twenty-eight rooms was decorated by a professional interior designer in a program we called 'Cat Cribs and Dog Digs.' Our goal was to create an environment that was welcoming and pleasant while educating visitors about our adoptable animals. Further, we wanted to foster the opportunity for prospective adopters to 'fall in love' and take home a pet because they felt a bond with the animal, not because they felt sorry for them. This gives a much better chance for an adoption to be long-term and the best scenario for everyone."

SDHS was at the forefront of animal welfare organizations. Following in the progressive footsteps of the San Francisco SPCA and Maddie's Pet Adoption Center, we were taking cues from others and building on them with our own ideas.

"We were fortunate to have Robert Wright, the president of the American Society of Interior Designers, volunteer to design a room for two of our wonderfully creative sponsors, Janie DeCelles and Vicki Baron," I continued. "In fact, the whole program germinated from their idea to have Robert contribute his talents to make over the dog room they sponsored. From there, the idea mushroomed into 'Cat Cribs and Dog Digs.' We ended up with twenty-eight different teams contributing over $250,000 of design and contracting services and materials for making our dog and cat quarters into designer living rooms, studios, and condominiums."

In truth, the program was so endearing and unique that it received the attention of the press and national television coverage. I got calls from colleagues around the country who lauded how creative we were and how much value we were adding to an adoption center. Then they politely, and sometimes not so politely, asked me to get off their local TV station so they could go back to garnering the elusive financial support so critical to their local shelter. Cat Cribs and Dog Digs was a classic example of the miracles possible when people are open to original ideas and share them with others catalyzing synergism and newfound potentials.

Over the next two hours with Wallis and Leonard, I continued as the tour guide through the rest of the campus, including a visit with our friends next door at the San Diego County Department of Animal Services. Led by Dawn Danielson, the County offered a variety of services that complemented the work done by SDHS.

"If anyone's interested, we can stop for lunch at the cafe," I suggested. That sounded good to everyone, so we adjourned to the front courtyard, where we could enjoy the beautiful day outside.

"Dr. Mark," Wallis said, "We're very impressed with what you've shown us today. It's obvious to me there's a lot of love and passion at work on this campus. Where do you see SDHS going from here?"

As we talked over lunch about programs to help foster the human-animal bond, it became clear that Wallis and Leonard not only wanted to see the campus facilities, but also were deeply interested in understanding our vision, goals, and challenges regarding our work in animal welfare. "Thank you so much for everything, Dr. Mark." Wallis warmly said. "You've been very generous in hosting our visit and sharing your thoughts with us. I know we've learned much that we can apply to our project."

At the airport, Wallis turned to me and, with her characteristic exuberance, said, "Dr. Mark, I want to say again how overjoyed I am to see the wonderful work SDHS is doing to help animals."

"Wallis, it was sincerely my pleasure," I replied. "I'm always happy to help any project whose goal is to strengthen the human-animal bond."

"As my way of saying thank you," she said, "I'd like to give you a gift."

I was surprised but immediately responded, "That was not the purpose of your trip. To me, it's gift enough that you made the effort to experience the campus and see what we've done in hopes it may inspire some ideas for your project in Los Angeles."

"It's because you did not ask that I want to acknowledge all the great work that's been done," she replied. "This is why I'm going to give SDHS $100,000." My shock must have been clearly evident because she looked at me and we both broke into tears of joy and hugged.

Over Wallis's shoulder, through my tears I saw Leonard, who had gone to find the pilot, returning into the waiting area. I thought of the unspoken rule in fundraising, to *never* approach the donor directly but go through the foundation and its application process. Without thinking, when I saw Leonard I involuntary exuded the first words out of my mouth: "I asked for nothing. I said nothing. And I did nothing. I promise!"

Leonard looked at Wallis and said with a smile, "What did you do now, Wallis?"

I was in shock but grateful for a random act of kindness that reminded me of the goodness of the world and the people who act to make the world a better place.

Wallis returned to Los Angeles and continued pursuing her dreams. Over the years, SDHS enjoyed her continued support, and we maintained a friendly relationship and shared interest in advocating for the welfare of the human-animal bond. The Annenberg Foundation even provided a grant to cover the work SDHS did in reuniting families and their dogs separated during Hurricane Katrina.

When the Annenberg Foundation proposed to develop a center

in Rancho Palos Verdes, I traveled north to speak to the town's planning commission on their behalf. The project became controversial and the foundation withdrew their proposal, but Wallis was undeterred. She moved on and formed collaborations with various Los Angeles organizations to design and construct a community space for animal welfare like no other.

After years of hard work, Wallis finally realized her dream when the Wallis Annenberg PetSpace opened in Playa Vista in 2017. Unlike many humane societies or traditional shelters that provide animal control, rescue operations, or similar services, Annenberg PetSpace is a state-of-the-art community center that focuses on education and pet adoptions. Through partnerships with shelters in the Los Angeles area, animals come to PetSpace to find their new family in a comfy and cheery environment.

Additionally, the facility serves the Wallis Annenberg PetSpace Leadership Institute. In 2001, Wallis's father Walter established The Annenberg Trust at Sunnylands, their unique estate home in Rancho Mirage, California. For decades, the couple hosted glamorous galas and holiday gatherings attended by the "Who's Who" in the top echelon of celebrity and political circles, from United States presidents to the Queen of England and Hollywood elites. With its own private golf course, fishing lake, and various amenities on the expansive grounds, Sunnylands was a natural haven for societal connections and a sphere of influence to impact the world at large. Walter created the foundation to ensure that Sunnylands would survive them as a place where thought leaders and heads of state alike could gather on neutral ground to share ideas and address issues facing the global community.

Continuing her father's legacy, Wallis wanted to provide a similar means for facilitating discourse in the study of the human-animal bond. Through the leadership institute, Annenberg

PetSpace will help to forge new approaches to fostering the human-animal relationship through interdisciplinary scholarship, policy discourse, and public education, in an atmosphere conducive to brainstorming and exploring common ground to needed solutions.

Annenberg PetSpace is a model for what is possible when passionate people persistently pursue their dreams in collaboration with others. I've seen this happen time and again in my career. When people and teams in the animal welfare world share ideas and learn from each other in a mode of cooperation—whether in shelters, zoos, or veterinary settings alike—the human-animal bond and our communities improve, sometimes in revolutionary ways. In sharing with Wallis the knowledge we had at SDHS, we helped to move the ball forward and extend the safety net for animals overall, just as we had years before in openly embracing ideas we received from the San Francisco SPCA, as well as zoos, veterinarians, and other inspirations. The world is a better place when we can share ideas and openly approach problems in new ways.

Ask Dr. Mark:

In These Challenging Times, What Is the Future of Animal Welfare?

When I relate stories of generous support given to the San Diego Humane Society, like Mrs. Harpst from Coronado, who wanted no thanks for her largesse, Margaret Cargill's gifts as an anonymous angel, or Wallis Annenberg's spontaneous act of kindness, inevitably there are cynics who say, "People like that do not exist anymore."

I'm fortunate to have witnessed overwhelming evidence to the contrary. Further, while it's easy to highlight stories of donors who have the resources to make spectacular financial contributions, I'm happy to report that such altruism exists across the spectrum of humanity irrespective of social status or financial ability.

During a Dog Walk event sponsored by the SDHS, I observed a homeless person receive money on a street corner from a passing stranger. With a bit of newfound change in his pocket, the beggared man came walking by the happenings at our event. When he found out it was a fundraiser to help animals, he immediately reached into his pocket, pulled out some coins, and put them in the donation jar. I went over and thanked him for his donation. The man smiled and cheerily responded, "Those little guys need it more than I do!"

In a society that can seem to put a skewed emphasis on material pursuits, we often don't hear about the kindness of a homeless person or the countless children who donate everything in their piggy bank to the local animal shelter. But the truth is, there are everyday heroes all around who freely give as much as they can to help, often with no thought for thanks, and do so even if their means are meager.

During the decade I served as CEO and president of the SDHS, on a daily basis I was blessed to experience random and planned acts of kindness and generosity. From small events with a donation jar up to our annual grand gala, the FurBall, I saw people from all walks of life donating not only their hard-earned money but also their time. In fact, SDHS volunteers contributed over 1 million hours of time in the course of my tenure, the equivalent of 25,000 weeks or 480 years. And this doesn't count the Girl Scout troop that spent a year learning how to quilt and then presented SDHS with its handcrafted art made to adorn the wall of our new campus with beautiful depictions of the human-animal bond.

Beyond the SDHS, I believe the importance given to animal welfare by society at large has increased exponentially over time, not only reflected by the donor community but, if you look for them, in many other areas.

Throughout the world, there is incrementally stronger legislation to better support animal welfare: laws that not only prohibit such abhorrent acts as dogfighting, cockfighting, puppy mills, and torturing animals but elevate such crimes to felonies. Even such unnecessary and painful procedures as declawing cats and docking tails and ears are prohibited in many jurisdictions. Similarly, regulations and policies have provided more stringent and careful management of natural habitats and protection of wildlife populations.

Companies are also retooling business processes in favor of more humane treatment of animals in developing products, researching medicines, and producing food.

Where only two decades ago, the thought of an animal visiting a patient in the hospital was unacceptable because of the possibility of "germs," today, healthcare facilities cannot get enough pet-assisted therapy programs to satisfy the emotional and physical needs of their patients.

In the wake of Hurricane Katrina in 2005, many families refused to evacuate their homes unless their animals could come with them. Some even made the ultimate sacrifice of dying with their pets instead of abandoning them. The world saw iconic pictures of disaster victims stranded on the rooftops of houses and cars, holding signs that read, "Please save us all!" to include their animal companions. Those images not only captured our hearts but also catalyzed a cultural change in the years that followed.

The Department of Homeland Security and the Centers for Disease Control and Prevention (CDC) recognized that family animals were no longer to be considered "pestilence" during an emergency, but were victims that needed help. Community emergency evacuation plans were rewritten to include how and who offers assistance to animals affected by catastrophic events. In fact, today federal funding for disaster preparedness is contingent on a community having an evacuation plan for companion animals during disasters.

The technology sector has developed advanced tools to protect our pets, such as GPS trackers to help find them when they're lost, and medical devices that let people know when their animals are showing signs of illness. Earlier intervention increases the chances of successful treatment and outcomes, and in turn, better health and longer lives for animals.

In caring for the health of animals, the medical community has even developed practical methods and a culture for reducing fear in pets when they visit a veterinarian. Exemplified by the Fear Free™ program founded by "America's Veterinarian," Dr. Marty Becker, the protocol of knowledge and tools help veterinary professionals and pet owners prevent and alleviate anxiety and stress in animals before, during, and after veterinary visits.

Since I began my journey decades ago as a young boy who loved animals, the importance of the human-animal bond has been brought to the forefront as one of the crucial social issues to be addressed in creating and maintaining a humane world. In weaving such values and support for the animal welfare into the fabric of our communities, there are very few social movements that can claim similar success.

When it comes to supporting our animal welfare organizations such as SDHS, in working closely with benefactors like the Annenberg or Margaret Cargill foundations, I came to understand the long hours of investigation, research, and due diligence that institutional staff and donors do to ensure their humanitarianism has a maximum positive impact. The epiphany I had was that it could even be more difficult for a foundation to responsibly provide financial resources to well-intentioned programs than it was for an organization to apply for them. Because of this, I have always thought of the well-known philanthropist, Miss Ellen Browning Scripps, and her philosophy in supporting various charitable endeavors. Miss Scripps claimed never to have "donated" money to a worthy cause. Instead, she "invested" in them. The return on her investments were not financial gains or notoriety. The dividends were the work accomplished and the impact on improving lives.

In forty years of working professionally and successfully raising over one hundred million dollars to strengthen the human-animal bond, I have seen innumerable acts of selfless kindness and support. I believe that as a species we humans not only value the unconditional love we receive from animals, but we also provide it in return on a daily basis.

Advancements in animal welfare ultimately not only depend on having the resources to do it, but having dedicated, competent staff and individuals in leadership positions to do the hard work. In the last three decades, I have experienced a significant effort to educate and provide excellent training to produce the leaders of today and tomorrow. An inspirational example of this is the certification of animal welfare administrators (CAWA certification) offered by the Association of Animal Welfare Advancement (AAWA). AAWA is a national organization with over 1,000 members dedicated to raising the bar of competent, caring individuals dedicated to saving the lives of all adoptable and treatable animals that enter our animal welfare campuses.

At the same time, I believe there is more work to do. Some of this work includes finding common ground between people on opposite sides of the debate spectrum, especially voices blinded by a fervor that polarizes others and stalls forward progression. While certain points of disagreement may never come together, life has taught me the wisdom of putting aside differences and doing our best to build commonality, motivated by a shared love of animals, and guided by the words of Mahatma Gandhi: "The greatness of a nation and its moral progress can be judged by the way its animals are treated."

It will take hard work and great dedication, but I see a bright future for animal welfare.

Ren had eyes that mirrored her kind and gentle soul.

Chapter 24

REN

I hung up the phone and nearly collapsed. Although my father was eighty-seven years old and had physical and mental health issues, the news of his death blindsided me in a wake of overwhelming devastation. I managed to make my way to a chair and sank deep into the cushions in a slumping sadness. My near-comatose state was suddenly broken when my dog Ren jumped onto my lap.

Ren was a mixed breed dog, a veritable canine cocktail with a shot of beagle and a jigger of Jack Russell terrier thrown in for good luck. This meant she normally had three speeds: running, talking, and sleeping. But at this moment, she uncharacteristically settled into another mode as she lay her head on my belly. I looked down to see her peering up at me with eyes that seemed to say, "It will be all right." On this day of profound sadness, Ren calmly sat with me for what seemed like hours as I absorbed the meaning of my loss and grieved. She was my source of strength.

When I was a young boy, I had wanted a dog more than anything, but my mother made it clear that she didn't care to have a messy fur ball running around the house. As I grew older, my dream of having a dog didn't abate one iota. When I turned thirteen and, in the Jewish tradition, considered responsible for my decisions and actions, I decided to give it another shot and ask for a dog at my bar mitzvah. Much to my surprise and delight, my mom gave in. Soon after, a beautiful Belgian sheepdog joined our family home.

I named the dog "Blackie" for his jet-black coat—descriptive, but perhaps not the most creative name I could have come up with—and he became my closest friend and constant companion. He knew more about my inner thoughts and fears than any other living being in my life.

Since my mother wasn't a "dog person," I never expected her to warm up to Blackie, but as time went by I knew her heart had been won over, signified by moments when she'd give the dog a *shissel*, or bowl, of ice cream. Or my dad would throw Blackie a piece of bagel, and my mother would scold, "How could you give that to him without some butter or cream cheese?" These thoughts popped into my mind as I sat with Ren in my lap, trying to come to terms with the fact that my father was gone.

Somewhat like Blackie, Ren came to live with our family as a result of child-parent negotiations, in this case with my younger daughter, Nicole. The bargaining originated while our family was living in the Bay Area in Northern California. I was working at the San Francisco SPCA when I received an offer to take the helm of the San Diego Humane Society in 2001 as president and CEO.

I was thrilled about the job opportunity. The organization had an excellent reputation in the community, and with its leadership, staff, and volunteers, I felt it had a bright future.

My wife Kris and I were excited about the prospect of moving to San Diego. When we first met, during our initial conversation, we agreed that San Diego would be an ideal place to live because of its near-perfect weather and opportunities for sailing and other out-door adventures. After we were married, we set a goal of someday living in San Diego's heavenly coastal region, so this was a chance to fulfill that dream.

However, for Nicole, the thought of moving was a travesty. "Mom and Dad," Nicole implored, "I've already moved from Boston to Los Angeles, then Los Angeles to San Francisco. I'm in high school now, and I don't want to go anywhere else." She was right. We had left Boston for California when I was offered the job as Director of the LA Zoo, then during her middle school years, we moved to San Francisco for an opportunity to work at the San Francisco SPCA. "On top of that," Nicole continued, "Lauren's going off to college, so it will just be me at the house. I won't know anyone at school, and my sister will be gone, too."

I thought back to my childhood. I felt fortunate my parents had stayed in one place throughout my schooling, but I felt just as blessed in having Blackie as my best friend during my teenage years. The bond between a teenager and a dog is magical and runs deep. I believe, in part, because the young adult has a confidant, they can tell anything to and feel accepted and safe. When the pressures of high school get the best of them, teens can go home to their best friend, who is never critical, and provides unconditional love.

"Nicole, I know some of this doesn't feel fair or easy to you, but what would you think if we adopted a dog once we're in San Diego?"

"Really? Do you mean it?" she perked up at the thought. At the time, we just had tortoises and geckos as pets—certainly different companionship than what a dog could provide.

"Yes, we mean it," Kris and I replied as one. "You can even pick it out. We promise." And so it was settled. Our family would move to San Diego where Kris and I would follow our lifelong dream of living in paradise, and Nicole would gain a new BFF (best *furry* friend) of her choosing.

I started my new job at the San Diego Humane Society, and Nicole began making numerous visits there in her search for the "right" dog. She knew the best way to identify the right one was to spend time interacting with many dogs at the shelter in a form of doggie "dating." I told her, "One day your eyes will meet with a specific animal and you'll know that's the one."

"Dad, come look," Nicole exclaimed with great excitement. "I found our dog!" I followed her out to the dog runs where Nicole pointed to an eight-week-old puppy who was fishing leaves out of a water dish with its little paw. Nicole said with a laugh, "Isn't she adorable, Dad? She's so cute and smart and funny. She has to be part of our family!" It seemed Nicole had found her soulmate. My daughter had fallen in love and, in truth, so had Kris and I. This little fur ball had captured our hearts, and we knew we had found our new family member.

When Nicole was a toddler, she had a hard time saying her sister's name, Lauren, so "Ren" became Lauren's nickname. With her sister going off to college, Nicole chose the name Ren for her new pup as she would help fill the void of her sister leaving home.

Nicole and Ren became inseparable. Kris and I may have paid for Ren's care, but the dog's loyalty was to her best friend, Nicole. If Nicole was in the house, Ren was right beside her. The bond between them deepened throughout all of Nicole's high school years and was a special relationship I wish every teenager could experience.

Time marches on, children grow up, and eventually it was time for my daughter to move on in life. Nicole left home and couldn't take Ren with her so, by proxy and given an animal's ability to adapt to change, Ren accepted Kris and me as the recipients of her engaging antics and unconditional love. In doing so, Ren became the unforeseen boon and rescue for filling the void of our empty nest. She would greet each of us at the door as if we had been gone for weeks, even if it was only a few hours. Whatever happened in the day, good or bad, when I came home Ren made me laugh. She had a keen sense for when it was okay to cause some mischief and when it was time to behave or knowing when her love and affection could act as much-needed consolation for life's dire moments.

Over the coming five years, the finale of Ren's life, I faced challenging health- and work-related issues that took a deep toll on me. Ren was always there with and for me during that critical time when I needed love and affection. She tirelessly consoled me, made me laugh, and on occasion, corrected me when I had moments of self-pity. She had wisdom and a voice.

One day, I heard the words no pet owner wants to hear. "I'm sorry, Mark," said Dr. Keith Richter, an exceptional veterinarian and friend. "It's confirmed. Ren has cancer throughout her liver." In my career, I spent over thirty years counseling people facing such prospects for their beloved animals, but it didn't come any easier for me.

This can't be happening, I thought, and then angrily wondered, *Why is this happening?* I felt helpless and vulnerable with grief pouring through me. I wanted to bargain a way to regain control, but as a veterinarian myself, I knew the realities of the prognosis. In a bittersweet way, Ren was giving me her last and most powerful lesson: *Mark, what you've been telling people all these years is true.*

I asked Dr. Richter questions as he explained the test results in more detail. I knew what lay ahead for my remarkable friend was terminal suffering, a future I would never wish for her. I knew in my heart the kindest thing I could do for Ren was to let her go. I then drove home with Ren and discussed everything with Kris and shared it with both of my daughters. We universally felt that the best decision was to afford her a peaceful passing.

I used to teach veterinary students that, when it comes to euthanizing an animal, it might be your second time conducting the procedure that day, but for the people losing their loved one, that pet is part of their family. In this critical moment, you're helping create a permanent memory for them. You can't make it joyful, but you can make it as painless as possible, because those moments of saying goodbye will be ones they remember the rest of their life.

Dr. Richter afforded us the beautiful opportunity of allowing Ren and me to be together for the last time by coming to our house. Everyone chooses differently to be present or not at the time of a loved one's passing. What's important is that it be done in an empathic and sensitive manner for all involved, with no judgement. I elected to hold Ren as Dr. Richter inserted the needle, and I sobbed as I felt her soul leave her body. She was at peace, but in that very profound and deeply emotional moment, at the same time I felt grateful to have had her in my life. Fortunately, Dr. Richter was a colleague whose approach to his practice was similar to my own. I'm forever grateful for his professionalism and kindness in helping me through one of the most difficult moments of my life, in the best possible way. Of all the times I had been through this process, it was my first time as the lamenting family member. The dog from my childhood, Blackie, passed away suddenly at the age of thirteen, so I was spared a similar moment of utter futility back then as there was no chance to think about it first or to help him through his passing.

It didn't matter that I intellectually understood the steps of grief; I still went through them. As time passed, I had moments where I felt Ren's presence in and around the house long after she was gone. I'd think I caught a glimpse of her out of the corner of my eye, or hear the sound of her nails clicking on the tile floor. Whether or not she was there in body, her spirit still filled our home, and her paw prints were forever on our hearts.

The best way I can think to memorialize her is with the words I wrote the night she passed away:

How fortunate we were to have Ren in our lives! All is quiet, and Ren is resting.

My heart is heavy with loss, but this loss is far outweighed by all the love and inspiration Ren shared unselfishly and unconditionally.

She made us laugh the first time we saw her, not realizing then how much Ren would bring to our lives over the years.

She was there when Nicole needed her the most, during those challenging teenage years.

She became frantic when we acted like adolescents.

She scolded us when we came home late. Of course, her definition of "late" was any time after at 5 PM or dinnertime.

She celebrated when we celebrated. Nobody could celebrate like Ren doing laps around the house, rejoicing even simple moments of someone's return from the mailbox. She taught us to love every moment that was free of fleas.

She used four-letter words when she was supposed to be quiet.

She was quiet when it mattered.

She sang arias while getting a bath.

She intimidated "Dr. Mark" so he couldn't examine her. She made us laugh when we were too serious.

She was a princess, but a benevolent one.

She showed us how to stand your ground. When it wasn't really necessary, you bark and then run home. But when it was time to stand your ground, she stood with all four paws.

She provided courage when we needed it most, and over the years that's been a lot. She reminded us to take every day one day at a time, and hope for your favorite food at the next meal.

She reminded us on a daily basis why we love animals so much, and that the work people do to strengthen the human-animal bond is important.

She exemplified loyalty, even when you clipped her nails, but if you gave Ren a pill, be careful; her loyalty was not to be taken for granted. She truly provided unconditional love.

Ren is missed, but not forgotten!

In the end, Ren taught me more than anyone but my parents. She was my own testament to the human-animal bond and its value and importance to each generation.

Chapter 25

MY LIFE OF LIVING THE BOND

 The lessons I've learned in life because I chose to be a veterinarian all came into focus while I watched a beautiful sunset over the Pacific blue ocean waters near my home. I was recovering from a recent major surgery, and, as I often do, I went to the beach to recharge my soul.

A few days earlier, while in the hospital to fuse five vertebrae in my neck, I was gifted several déjà vu moments from people filtering through my room wanting to know why "elephant accident" was listed as the reason for my having surgery. The experience transported me back to my youth in Florida when Donia, the Asian elephant whose story started this book, so easily tossed me like a rag doll through the air to defend her island territory and landed me in the hospital. The years hadn't changed people's curiosity about seeing "elephant accident" on a medical chart or their interest in hearing a good animal story.

Why is this? I believe the answer is simple: because people love animals.

When I've shared the story of my "encounter" with Donia, and related how I punched the great pachyderm matriarch in the eye hopefully to save my life, I've sometimes heard, "That's amazing Mark, but how was Donia's eye?" While I admittedly had a tinge of feeling insignificant when asked that question—I nearly died, not the elephant—in the end, I understand. There's something extraordinary about the human-animal bond. It's why I chose to become a veterinarian.

Many times people have told me, "Dr. Mark, you have the best job in the world. I once wanted to be a veterinarian, but then I realized I couldn't do it because I love animals too much!" Every veterinarian has heard similar comments at times in their career. "I just couldn't deal with seeing an animal die or watching them bleed."

From a certain point of view, such a remark is a bit strange in that it seems to suggest a veterinarian doesn't care as much about animals as the person stating it. Of course, this is categorically untrue. Intellectually, I appreciate that's not what the person intends to imply, yet the statement is illuminating in some ways.

Over the years, I have informally spoken to my colleagues who have pursued a veterinary career about their motivations for doing so. Invariably, they are driven by an overwhelming desire to make the lives of animals better and to have a positive impact on the people who care for those animals. But the reality isn't always unicorns and rainbows. A typical conversation starts like this: "Doctor, I want to do everything I can for our dog. He's a member of the family. My wife and children will be devastated if we can't fix . . . Wait a minute! It will cost *how* much?"

This scenario is repeated multiple times in a typical day in animal clinics and hospitals across the country. A veterinarian learns to expect this paradoxical challenge as the norm, where finances or other circumstances can be the controlling factors in determining the level of care given to an animal, or makes the vet a counselor to an owner that may have to choose between a costly procedure for their pet or another vital family need. On top of this, veterinarians earn less than physicians, because they charge less, have higher costs and crippling debt, and don't get reimbursed by insurance, so the financial burden can be heavy.

Another challenge veterinarians face in general practice is dealing with death nearly on a daily basis. For one, pets live shorter lives than humans, so it's simply a matter of the cycle of life. Compounding this further is that in the twenty or so appointments a vet has on any given day, invariably, at least one of them will be to euthanize a beloved family pet to spare them from unnecessary suffering.

Such circumstances can be emotionally demanding and are sometimes downright painful. They can crush a person's spirit. Recently, veterinarians earned the onerous distinction of having among the highest rates of suicide, both in the medical profession and compared to the general population. In fact, a recent study published in the *Journal of the American Veterinary Medical Association* showed that male veterinarians were 2.1 times more likely to die by suicide than the general population and female veterinarians 3.5 times more likely.

I too have had my crushing moments. What I would say to someone who may be struggling under the weight of their chosen profession is that you can choose to be taken down by the issues, or you can learn to make them a source of strength. From my experience and point of view, I believe that finding and stoking this strength is what enables you to make a positive difference. I can attest that after more than forty years of having this ability to heal, along with the responsibility to sometimes end a life, I feel blessed.

Given all this, I've sometimes been asked, "What would you choose for a career if you could do it all over again?" My unequivocal answer is I would choose to be a veterinarian. For me, it's been the best job in the world despite any hardships I faced along the way.

I would choose to work again with the great health professionals I was privileged to know, to serve side by side and learn from empathetic and talented animal care providers, and replicate all the interactions I've had with colleagues, clients, and the public. I would experience all over again each opportunity that helped me grow as a person and a doctor.

I would especially love to relive every chance I had to observe, study, examine, diagnose, treat, and hug every animal that crossed my path and helped teach me about life.

When I look back to one of my early lessons in life as taught by Donia, I think I was more convinced than ever that I wanted to dedicate my life to helping animals. I understood the elephant's behavior and that the events that almost ended my life were of my doing, so I chalked it up to a learning moment. It's a miracle that I survived, and for that I'm forever grateful.

It's just one in a series of miracles and "WOW" moments my life has been—a life of love and great adventure, one lived for the human-animal bond.

P.S. For those who are still wondering, *But how was Donia's eye?* I'm happy to report that Donia was just fine and suffered no injury.